Winning Basketball
For Girls

Winning Basketball
For Girls
(New Edition)

Faye Young Miller
and Wayne Coffey

Facts On File, Inc.

Winning Basketball for Girls
(new edition)

Facts On File, Inc.
11 Penn Plaza
New York NY 10001

Library of Congress Cataloging-in-Publication Data
Miller, Faye Young.
    Winning basketball for girls / Faye Young Miller and Wayne Coffey.
        p. cm.
    Rev. ed. of: Winning basketball for girls.
    Includes index.
    Summary: An introduction, in text and illustrations, to the
techniques and strategies of girl's basketball.
        ISBN 0-8160-2776-5 (alk. paper)
        1. Basketball for girls. {1. Basketball for girls.} I. Coffey,
Wayne R. II. Title.
GV 886.M48   1992
796.323'62—dc20   91-36937

Facts On File books are available at special discounts when purchased in bulk quantities for businesses, associations, institutions, or sales promotions. Please call our Special Sales Department in New York at 212/967-8800 or 800/322-8755.

You can find Facts On File on the World Wide Web at **http://www.factsonfile.com**

Cover design by Cathy Rincon

Printed in the United States of America

VB VC 10 9 8 7 6 5 4

This book is printed on acid-free paper.

Contents

Legend for Illustrations

O   Offensive player
X   Defensive player
●   Player with the ball
〜〜➤   Dribble
– – –➤   Pass
——➤   Cut

Enthusiasm is the electricity of life. How do you get it? You act enthusiastic until you make it a habit. Enthusiasm is natural; it is being alive, taking the initiative, seeing the importance of what you do, giving it dignity and making what you do important to yourself and to others.

—Gordon Parks, author and film director

Photo Credits

Acknowledgments

Thanks to my family for their love and especially to my mom for her support.

Thanks to my coaches for sharing such a wonderful game with me.

Thanks to my former teammates and players for all the experiences we shared together.

Thanks to Sheila, Beth, Karen, and my twin sister, Kaye, for their assistance in the photo sessions.

—F.Y.M.

Very special thanks to my brother, Frank, an estimable basketball coach and mentor, who taught me the finer points of shooting layups and sneaking into gyms; to the girls of the Horace Mann basketball teams (1979–83), who made basketball season a very special and much-awaited time; to Don Hamerman, a talented photographer with the patience of several saints; to Faye Young Miller, who was as cooperative as a collaborator as she was committed to making this book the best of its kind; and to Gerry Helferich, whose care and deft editorial hand were the book's shaping forces from the outset.

—W.C.

Introduction

Women's basketball hasn't grown. It has exploded. In the last two decades the number of girls playing interscholastic basketball has jumped more than 500 percent. Youth leagues have sprung up everywhere. The number of summer camps seems to double annually. More and more colleges are developing first-rate programs, and girls are playing at younger ages than ever before. Is it any wonder that players are getting better and better?

I've experienced the game's progress firsthand. When I started playing, more than twenty years ago, women's basketball bore little resemblance to what we see today. There were six players to a side—two on offense, two on defense, and two rovers. Only the rovers were free to roam all over the court. The other four players had to stay in their designated offensive or defensive area, a rule that did little to encourage all-around basketball skills. Worse still, in some parts of the country you were allowed only two dribbles before getting rid of the ball. Fortunately, the powers that be finally saw the folly in such a setup, and in 1971 a rule was passed allowing girls to play under boys' rules (except in Oklahoma and Iowa, where they still play six-a-side style). The women's game has been booming ever since.

It "boomed" for me right from the start, which was in seventh grade on my junior high school team in Bunn, North Carolina. It was the first time the school had a team, and the coach was scouting the corridors and classrooms for possible recruits. He took one look at my twin sister, Kaye, and me, noted we were 5-foot-7 (pretty tall for seventh-graders), and asked us to try out. We did, and for both of us, it was love at first shot . . . and dribble . . . and pass. . . . We went 8-0 that season, and Kaye and I haven't strayed far from the hardwood since.

I practiced two to three hours a day, year round, right through high school, college, and the pros. Being dedicated was easy for me; not only was it what I wanted to do, we also had a terrific high school team and I badly wanted to keep that tradition going. Maybe you've gotten hooked right away, as I did. Or maybe your interest has come along more slowly. Whether you're an eager beginner or a seasoned high school veteran, you must have the basketball bug by now if you're reading this book, and I think that's great. The more girls that play, the better the women's game will get. And that's only good for all of us, players and coaches alike.

I've written this book with two aims: one, to give you specific, straight-forward instruction—pointers and drills for improving every facet of your game; and two, to "talk" basketball with you in a broad sense, in a way that'll give you a better feel for the reasons behind what you're doing on the court. My years of coaching and playing have convinced me that in basketball the "whys" are nearly as important as the "hows." You'll often hear coaches talk about "muscle memory"—constantly repeating a particular drill until your body is programmed to perform it correctly. That's valuable, no doubt about it. But it's even more valuable when the movement is explained, so you understand *why* it's so important to execute it in that way. We could spend a practice session working on how to dribble, and it would be time well spent. So much the better, though, when we talk about the dribble as an offensive weapon, and where and when it should (and shouldn't) be used. Such insights will increase your feel for the game, and that's important. The best players aren't those who go out there with a mechanical, do-this, do-that approach, but those who develop a court sense of how and when to move and react on the floor in different situations.

My sister Kaye and I were co-captains of North Carolina State (1977–78), the state champion and third-ranked team in the nation. (That's me on the right.)

The point is that getting to know the game better as you learn to play it better will make a huge difference in your rate of improvement. So will having the right attitude.

Any coach can tell you how important attitude is to a player's development. One of the biggest frustrations for a coach is having a talented player who, for whatever reason, doesn't concentrate or push herself to improve. One of the greatest satisfactions, on the other hand, is seeing a girl of limited natural talent work hard to become the best basketball player she can be. The way you approach the game will have a big effect on how well you play it.

Be Enthusiastic

In this book, we'll talk a lot about working hard and improving, but don't forget that the most important guideline of all is to enjoy yourself when you're playing. That, presumably, is why you picked up the ball in the first place, and why you're continuing to play. This book is intended to be a means to that end. After all, the better you play, the more fun it'll be.

As long as basketball is fun, you'll naturally be enthusiastic about it, and that makes any experience more fulfilling. Show enthusiasm when you play. Play with spirit. Congratulate your teammate when she makes a nice play. Support the others and pick them up when they're down. Praise unselfish play—the pass or the screen that can easily go unnoticed. Say "Nice try" if a teammate attempts a move that doesn't work out as planned. Admit your mistake when you've missed an open man or made a bad play. Don't bad-mouth other players, grumble about practice, or complain publicly about the coach. If you're not enjoying yourself or you feel as though you're being mishandled, talk to your coach about it. She'll want to know.

You don't have to be a full-time cheerleader. Not everybody is suited to the rah-rah stuff. Enthusiasm is a state of mind. And the best thing about it—besides how much it enhances your enjoyment—is what it does for others. Enthusiasm is contagious. It can spread through a team in no time. It'll keep everybody closely knit, foster a spirit of cooperation, and lift you up when you're not having one of your more memorable practices or games.

If you've played on a team where enthusiasm was the watchword, none of this is new to you. If you haven't, please take it on faith that being positive and showing enthusiasm will make your basketball experiences infinitely more rewarding—as a player and as a person. "Nothing great was ever achieved without enthusiasm," said Ralph Waldo Emerson. No argument here.

Now let's hit the court.

Faye Young Miller

Atlanta, Georgia

Winning Basketball For Girls

Chapter One

A Look at the Game

Just over a century ago in Springfield, Massachusetts, a physical-education instructor named Dr. James Naismith was looking for a game that could be played indoors in the cold winter months. He fastened two peach baskets to the gymnasium balcony and told his students to try throwing a soccer ball into the baskets. Thus was basketball born.

In the game's infancy, there were no backboards. No dribbling was allowed, and seven persons played on a team. There wasn't even an open basket; a person had to sit atop a ladder to pull the ball out of the basket and toss it back down to the players. Gradually changes and refinements were made until the game evolved into the game we know today. Let's get a quick overview of that game before we get into our more in-depth discussion of specific skills and instruction.

The Court

Most high school basketball courts are 84 feet long by 50 feet wide. College courts are the same width, but 94 feet long. A basket, consisting of a rim (a steel hoop 18 inches in diameter) and a backboard (a piece of Plexiglas or wood measuring 4 feet by 6 feet), is 10 feet from the ground at either end of the playing area.

The court is divided by a midcourt line, and is marked off by baselines (at each end of the court) and sidelines, as shown in Fig. 1.1. Fifteen feet out from the baselines are the free-throw or foul lines, where a player shoots an uncontested shot after an opponent commits a foul.

The Court

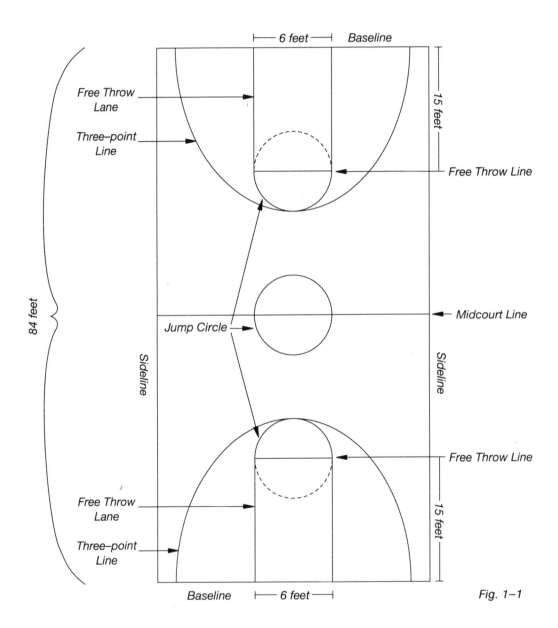

Fig. 1–1

A 6-foot-wide area between the foul line and the basket (it's usually painted) is known as the "key," free-throw lane, or three-second area, so named for a rule that prohibits any offensive player from staying in it for more than three seconds at a time. At the center of the court is a jump circle, where the official tosses up the ball to start the game.

The Players

Basketball is played by two teams of five players each. The basic positions include a center, two forwards, and two guards. The center, usually the tallest player on the team, generally stays closer to the basket than the other players, setting up in the area of the free-throw lane. If the center is positioned near the free-thrown line, she's known as a high post; if she's positioned close to the baseline, she's known as a low post. The forwards, sometimes known as wings, play a little farther out, usually to the sides of the basket. Along with the center, they are the main rebounders on the team.

The guards set up farthest out. They are traditionally agile players who are good ball-handlers and well-suited to setting up plays from their position. On many teams, one player is designated as the point guard, who handles the ball most of the time and is the quarterback of the offense. The other guard is called the shooting guard and is relied on for perimeter shooting and passing. Because of their distance from the basket, and because they have to stay back to guard against a fast break, guards tend to get fewer rebounds than forwards and centers.

How the Game Is Played

The team with possession of the ball is known as the offensive team; the other is the defensive team. Points are scored by shooting the ball into the basket being defended by the opposing team. Each team can score only by shooting at the opponent's basket, which is why the game flows up and down the court.

Two or three points are awarded for a successful shot, depending where it's taken from. These shots are called field goals. To get credit for three points, a player must be behind the three-point line, which is 19 feet, 9 inches from the hoop. One point is awarded for a successful free throw, or foul shot, a shot taken from the free-throw line after a foul by an opposing player. Not all fouls result in free throws, however. To go to the line, a player must be fouled in the act of shooting, or fouled intentionally. The other instance when free throws are taken is when the defensive team has surpassed its allotted number of fouls—over the limit, as it's called. Common fouls include pushing, reaching in, holding, and hitting a player's arm as she's shooting. After five fouls, a player is disqualified from the game.

Common sense tells us that the closer to the basket a shot is attempted, the better the chances that it will go in. The objective of the offensive team is to advance the ball so as to get the best shot that it can. There are only two ways the ball can be advanced—passing (throwing it from one player to another) or dribbling (bouncing the ball as you move in any direction).

The defensive team's objective is to protect the basket by keeping the offense as far from it as possible. Ideally, the defensive team wants to stop the offense from even attempting a shot. The next best thing is forcing them to take a difficult or low-percentage shot.

Whenever a shot is missed, players on both teams compete to get the rebound. Once the defensive team gets possession of a rebound, they go on offense and the other team goes on defense. In women's basketball, an offensive team has 30 seconds in which to attempt a shot. If they fail to do so, the other team gets possession of the ball.

Many complicated strategies and playing patterns are involved as the offense and defense try to accomplish their goals. For example, a team might play man-to-man defense, in which each player is assigned a player to guard; or it might play a zone defense, in which each player is assigned an area of the court to defend. Some teams play a combination of these two defenses or switch from one to another during a game. Another defensive option is to guard a team over the full length of the court, instead of just as they approach the basket. Full-court defense is often employed late in a game when the defensive team is losing and needs to catch up in a hurry.

There are an equal number of offensive strategies that a team might use to get through the defense and gain good shots at the basket. At this point it's not important for you to know the technical ins and outs of various playing schemes and patterns. What is important is to get a basic understanding of the game and of what you need to do on the court to play it as well as you can. And that's where we're headed for the rest of this book.

Chapter Two

Getting Started

Seeing yourself improve provides one of the biggest satisfactions in basketball. You make more shots than you did the month before. You pull down more rebounds. You play better defense, and you turn the ball over fewer times. As your command of the fundamentals gradually gets better, you feel good about your accomplishments, and you want to continue striving for more.

Making progress keeps you going. Let's look at what you can do to make as much of it as possible.

Basketball 101

I learn something new every time I watch a game. You can, too. Take in as many games as possible, whether it's the pros on TV or the JV boys in the next gym. Try to analyze the strategies involved. What kind of defense is being played? What are the players doing to get open? Which team is taking the higher percentage shots? Is one team dominating the play under the boards? Look at the players other than the one with the ball. Are they moving or standing still? Are they making the defense work? What about the tempo of the game? Is one team fast-breaking and the other playing deliberately? Look for good free-throw shooters; what are they doing that you might emulate? Is there one player doing most of the scoring? If so, what is she doing to get free for her shots? Where are her shots coming from? What fakes is she using?

Watching basketball is the next best thing to playing it. You'll get a much clearer perspective of the game by watching others play—and that'll translate, slowly but surely, into a crisper, more intelligent game for you. Say you're watching a game in which a guard continually puts the ball on the floor the moment she gets it, and winds up getting stuck—tied up or double-teamed by the defense because she no longer can use the dribble to get away. It's a terrific way to learn why you shouldn't waste your dribble.

Take a Self-Inventory

You know your own game—your strengths and weaknesses—better than anybody else. Even if you're just starting to play, take an inventory of yourself as a player and jot it down. Be honest. Write down what you need to work on most. This is a good way to emphasize what areas to concentrate on, as well as to chart your progress. Check back periodically. Measure how effective your practice has been in improving your problem areas.

This might seem obvious, but you'd be surprised how many players *don't* work on their weaknesses. I'm not denying it's a lot more fun to practice what you're already good at. But it's also fun to improve. Break down the game into categories and take notes on each. Here's the way it might look:

Dribbling: Right hand pretty good. Left hand needs a lot of work. Unable to dribble under control with head up.

Shooting: Lay-ups pretty good from right side, poor from left; need to work on improving speed and control from right, form and accuracy from left. Foul shooting averaging out at 50 percent. Outside shooting very inconsistent—one day on, one day off. Need to work on shooting the same way every time.

You get the idea. Be honest; it's the only way you'll really know how you're progressing.

Get the Most out of Practice Time

John Wooden, probably the most respected basketball coach of all time, once said, "You play the way you practice." If you play halfheartedly and develop sloppy habits in your driveway or schoolyard, it's going to carry over into your games. Make the most of your practice time. This doesn't mean it has to be totally structured; I only mean you have to practice diligently if you want to improve. Work all the different skill areas. Develop your own routines, but vary them so you keep it interesting. Maybe you'll designate one day as "Dribble Day," and you'll put a special emphasis on controlling the ball. Be imaginative. Dribble down your driveway with your left hand and come back using your right. Set up obstacles and dribble in and out of them. Get your little brother and follow him around as you dribble with your head up. On another day, maybe you'll arrange a shooting contest between two imaginary teams. Or set specific shooting goals and try to meet them. One day maybe you'll aim to make 10 of 20 eight-foot bank shots. As soon as you do, give yourself another goal to shoot for.

Keep pushing to improve. Concentrate on doing things right. But at the same time, inject some twists and games into your routine so your time on the court is always interesting and challenging. The best practices are fun *and* constructive.

Play "Up"

The surest and fastest way to improve is by playing with better players. It may be discouraging at first, but playing slightly over your head will work wonders for you. It offers a close-up view of how better players shoot, dribble, pass, cut, play defense, and so on, and it'll give you insights into what you have to do to take your game a notch higher. If you've never been able to steal the ball from the girl you've been guarding, she must be doing a good job of protecting the ball. Pay attention to how she does it.

Playing "up" forces you to push yourself, to work a little harder and play a little smarter. It gives you new goals to shoot for and will help you reach a higher skill level. It's great fun to team up with a friend and whip two younger girls down the street, 15-2, but what do you really get out of that? Complacency is big trouble for any reasonably competitive athlete. You have to want to continue improving. We all need an incentive to keep working at it, and playing up is that incentive.

I know a girl who, as a freshman JV player, stayed after practice every day and played with two of her coaches and a varsity player. She was taught a lot of hard lessons for a while and went home discouraged more than once. But how she improved! She began that season as a reserve on the JV. A year later, she was a starter on the varsity.

Ask Questions

Be curious about the game. If you don't understand your coach's advice or instruction, ask her about it. Most coaches like questions because it forces them to refine their own thinking, and shows them you're eager to learn. Say, for instance, the coach says to get "more leg" into your shot. Maybe you're thinking, "What's the big deal? I shoot with my arms, not my legs." But when you ask her, she explains that much of the power needed to get a shot smoothly up to the basket is generated by the legs, and that's why it's important to bend them before you begin your shooting motion. Knowing the reason for performing certain moves makes it easier to remember them.

Also ask questions of other players, particularly those you admire. ("How do you make that crossover dribble?" "Why do you catch passes that way?") Every little insight you collect will contribute to your improvement.

Chapter Three

Getting in Shape

Basketball is a vigorous game. Most high school courts, as indicated earlier, are 50 feet wide and 84 feet long and college courts are ten feet longer. That's a lot of hardwood to cover in 32 or 40 minutes, respectively. In fact, in an average game you'll log about three miles—virtually all of it in quick, demanding bursts.

You must be in good physical condition to play basketball. There's no way around it. If you're not in good shape, the game won't be as much fun because you won't be as effective. You might feel okay in the first or second quarter, and halftime might recharge you some, but as the game moves into the second half you're going to be in deep trouble. Fatigue sets in and form moves out, and the result is that all the techniques and fundamentals that come naturally when you're rested suddenly desert you. Passes get sloppy, shots bounce off the front of the rim (if they get to the basket at all), and defense is reduced to token resistance.

There's only one way to avoid this physical deterioration, and that is to get into prime basketball condition. That means getting your body toned for sharp cuts and changes of direction, quick starts and stops, repeated jumping without becoming nailed to the floor, and constant flexing of the legs. It also means strengthening your hands and getting a good feel for the ball.

Treating Your Feet Well

As a basketball player, you'll be only as good as your feet feel, which means you've got to take good care of them. Neglecting your feet can hamper your performance all season long.

Begin caring for your feet by putting them in a good pair of sneakers. I can't recommend a brand name because different sneakers fit each foot differently. If you've had any ankle trouble at all, get high-cut sneakers, which give extra support. Otherwise, let your feet be the judge. Try on several different pairs and see which feels best. Look for a sturdy sole, a well-cushioned arch, and strong construction along the edge where the sole meets the body of the shoe. That's where basketball shoes are most likely to tear.

As with most everything else, you get what you pay for with sneakers. Cheap brands not only are a bad investment, they're potentially dangerous because they're not built for heavy-duty basketball wear, or to give your feet the support they need. This is the era of the $100 (and up!) basketball shoe. Do you have to go that far? Not at all. Plenty of quality shoes can be had for far less. My advice is simply to invest in a good pair. They're worth it—and so are you. Besides, basketball is an inexpensive game. You'll have hardly any other expenses.

It's also a good idea to wear two pairs of socks to guard against blisters. This is particularly true early in the season, when your feet aren't accustomed yet to the pounding they're taking. Make sure you pull the socks all the way on and smooth out places where they're bunching up. Even a slight irritant like a bunched-up sock can result in a painful blister.

Conditioning Your Hands

A former coaching colleague of mine always used to tell his players, "Your hands and your feet are your career." And he is so right. We've looked at a few basic ways to care for your feet. With your hands, there are two important considerations—strength and feel for the ball—and they come into play in almost all facets of the game: catching, passing, shooting, dribbling, and rebounding. The stronger your hands, the more crisply you'll be able to play. Passes will be sharper. Shooting range will be better. You'll hang onto tough rebounds that other players might lose. Developing a soft (or sensitive) touch for the ball is equally important. It'll allow you to shoot and pass more accurately, dribble with more control, and handle the ball quickly without fumbling. Following are some drills and exercises for the hands.

Pounding the Ball

Here's a good way to get your hands familiar with the ball. Hold the ball near your shoulder in one hand and "pound" it firmly into the other with a forceful overhand throwing motion. Then pound it back to the hand you started with, and go back and forth 25 times. Concentrate on feeling the ball as you pound it into your receiving hand.

Squeezing a Ball

You can do this anytime, anywhere. Squeeze a sponge-rubber ball, hard, in one hand 25 times, then switch hands and squeeze out another 25. Continue until you've done 50 with each hand. It won't take long, and it's a terrific way to build strength in your hands and wrists.

Around the World

Fig. 3–1   Around the world. Move the ball as quickly as you can around your waist, concentrating on developing a good feel for the ball and on maintaining good control.

Start with the ball at waist level, holding it with both hands. Take the ball in your right hand and carry it around behind your back until it's almost to your left hip. At that point take it with your left hand, swing it around in front of you until it's almost to your right hip, then switch back to the right hand. Move the ball as quickly as you can in this circular motion without losing control. Continue whipping the ball "around the world" 20 times to your right. Then do another 20 to the left.

Figure-8 Drill

Flex your knees and move your feet out so they're at least a foot wider than your shoulders. Do not lean or bend from the waist as shown in Fig. 3–2. Holding the ball with both hands, begin with it between your legs, at about knee level. Then, shifting the ball to your right hand, move it inside and behind your left knee and pick it up there with your left hand. Swing it around in front of your left knee, then back through the legs to behind the right knee, where you shift it back to the right hand. Swing it around front again, and keep going until you've done 15 Figure 8's. Then do another 15, beginning in the same place, but this time start by moving the ball in front of your left knee. In this drill, too, move the ball as fast as you can without losing control.

Fig. 3–2   Figure-8 drill

Fingertip Control

Hold the ball in front of you about chest-high and quickly tap it back and forth between the pads of your fingers. Gradually raise your arms, lightly tapping the ball as you go, until the ball is directly overhead. Keep tapping, and slowly bring your arms down to the original position. Repeat five times. Your arms should start almost straight (keep just a slight flex in the elbows) and stay that way throughout the drill.

The Importance of Stretching

Most athletic injuries result from improper warm-up or lack of flexibility. Flexibility is the range of motion in a joint or combination of joints. Poor flexibility causes poor movement, which causes muscles to work harder. This in turn causes a greater loss of energy, and hinders your court performance. Taking time and care to stretch out decreases your chance of injury and increases your body's efficiency.

How to Stretch

Young muscles aren't as prone to pulling or straining as older muscles, but why risk it? Here are some pointers for stretching safely and properly:

- Concentrate on the muscle being stretched.
- Be positive. Stretch with a relaxed and open mind.
- Stretch to the point where it's still comfortable, not painful. Straining keeps the muscle from relaxing.
- Don't bounce. This actually tightens the muscle and can lead to injury. Extend yourself slowly and hold that position for at least 20 seconds.
- Breathe with a slow, normal rhythm. Don't hold your breath.
- Stretch after a very light warm-up. First, shoot around for a few minutes, take some lay-ups—loosen up just a bit so that the muscles aren't ice cold when you begin stretching.
- Stretch both before and after every workout. Muscles contract after they've been exercised, so it's important to stretch them back out when you're done.

Here are some stretches to work on:

Tricep Stretch

Pull your left elbow behind your head, using your right arm to stretch the tricep muscle (the back part of your upper arm) and the top of the shoulder. Hold, then switch arms.

Side Stretch

Standing with your hands straight over your head, bend sideways from the waist and lower your right arm down toward your right knee. Follow it with your left arm, slightly bent and just behind your head. Feel the stretch at your side; don't cheat by bending forward. Hold, and repeat on the other side.

Up and Over

This stretches the lower back and hamstrings. Lie on your back, raise both legs up and over your head and try to touch the floor with your toes. Place your hands on your hips for support. Keep the legs straight for maximum stretch. Hold 10 seconds, lower the legs, and repeat three times.

Spinal Twist

This exercise stretches the muscles along the spine and on each side of the hips as well as the arms. Starting in a seated position on the floor with your legs straight, take your left leg, cross it over your right knee, and place your left foot flat on the floor. With your right arm, reach around your bent leg as if trying to grab your left hip. Take the left arm and put it behind you as you slowly turn your head toward your left shoulder. Hold. Then cross the right leg over your left, and repeat the same stretch on the right side.

Butterfly

Sit on the floor and, with the soles of your feet together, grab your ankles or your toes. Gently pull yourself foward, using your elbows to *slowly* push your knees toward the ground. This stretch is primarily for the groin muscles, which are used so much in basketball, especially on defense.

Fig. 3–3 The butterfly. For extra stretch, use your elbows to gently push your knees toward the floor.

Hurdler's Stretch

Sit on the floor, with one leg bent beside you, the other straight out in front as shown in Fig. 3–4. Keeping your leg straight and your knee on the floor, slowly bring your chest down toward your knee. Hold the position. This stretches your hamstring muscles in the back of the leg. Now lean back as far as you can (you may need to use your opposite elbow to hold you up) and hold it, feeling the stretch in the quadriceps muscles in the front part of your bent leg. Switch legs and repeat.

Calf Stretch

To stretch the calf muscles and the Achilles tendons in the back part of your lower legs, stand facing a wall at arm's length with your heels on the floor and your back straight. Reach out and touch the wall, then slowly back your legs away from it to maximize the stretch. Make sure the heels stay on the ground throughout the exercise.

Fig. 3–4 The hurdler's stretch. The first part *(top)* stretches the hamstring muscle in the back of the leg. Make sure to keep the extended leg straight, and bring your chest as far forward toward your knee as you can. The second part of this exercise *(bottom)* stretches the quadriceps of your bent leg.

The Conditioners

Here are some of my favorite exercises for getting in shape for basketball. Perform these regularly for at least a month before the season, and I promise you'll show the coach something special when tryouts roll around. Even if you don't make a shot all day, your conditioning will make you stand out from the pack. Coaches love players who can run . . . and run . . . and run. . . .

Distance Running

Run long distances at least twice a week. Depending on your condition, you might start with a half mile or mile. Gradually work up to two miles. Keep track of your times. As you get in better condition, you'll find you can maintain a faster pace. If you can run two miles in 18 minutes or under, you're doing fine.

Basketball Sprints

Sprints are especially useful close to tryouts because they approximate the running you'll be doing on the court. Measure a distance of about 30 yards (roughly the length of a court). Sprint as hard as you can over the distance, then gradually slow down by jogging a few steps. Rest about three times the length of time you exercised; thus, if the sprint takes you seven seconds, rest for about 20. On the return trip, backpedal as fast as you can, and use the same formula for rest. Make three back-and-forth sprints. Not only is this great for your stamina, it's also valuable because the backpedaling improves your balance and conditions you for games, when you'll be doing a lot of that.

Wall Sit

You can do this one anywhere you have a wall. Leaning against it with your back straight, drop into a sitting position so your legs are at an angle of a little more than 90 degrees. Hold it for 15 seconds to start. Work up

Fig. 3–5 Wall sit. When you do this properly, you will feel the stretch in the fronts of your thighs (the quadriceps).

to 60 seconds. If that becomes easy, continue increasing the time. Doesn't sound too tough, does it? Try it—you'll be in for a surprise. Holding this position is a lot harder than you think. This is a good way to work your quadriceps, the large muscles in the front of your thighs. They've got to be in good shape to play good defense.

Jumping Rope

One of the finest conditioning drills going, jumping rope improves agility, footwork, upper-body strength, hand coordination, and endurance. Begin by jumping for three minutes without stopping, and work up to ten. Stay relaxed and develop a nice, easy rhythm, with no bounces between skips. Vary your steps, jumping with two feet, then alternating feet (i.e., 10 with the right, 10 with the left), jogging in place, jumping side to side, and jumping backward.

Harvard Step

Find a step or bench about 10 inches high. Step up with your right foot, bring up your left, step down with your right, followed by your left. Repeat as many full cycles as you can in 30 seconds, then repeat starting with your left leg. This is a demanding exercise, and great for strengthening your legs.

Box Drill

Draw or tape a box (about three feet square) on the ground with four equal compartments. With your feet together, jump clockwise from one box to the next for 30 seconds, facing forward at all times. Rest, then repeat for 30 seconds jumping counterclockwise.

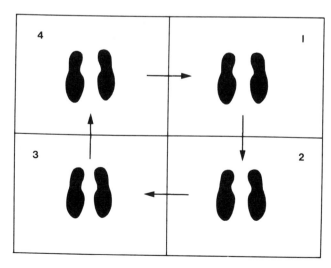

Fig. 3–6 The box drill. Note that the feet always point in the same direction.

Both Knees Up

Strengthening your lower abdominal muscles is an important part of getting in shape for basketball. These muscles get a lot of work from all the starts, stops, pivots, and jumps made on the court. To condition the lower abdominals, lie on the foor with your hands tucked under your rear end. Start with your legs straight out, just a few inches off the ground, and slowly raise your legs, and bend your knees in toward your chest. Lower them back, never letting the legs touch the floor. Repeat ten times.

About Weight Training

More and more in recent years, competitive women's basketball programs—in high school as well as college—have been using weight training to aid in the overall conditioning of their players. I put my team at Manhattan College through a rigorous program, and the results were tremendous. Players were able to jump higher, run harder without tiring, pass and rebound better—I think it improved nearly every aspect of the team's game. Aerobics and other conditioning classes have also become popular. The combination of aerobics and weight training is the ideal for pre-season conditioning.

I won't go into specific weightlifting routines and exercises here. However, if you are interested in giving weight training a try, talk to your coach or trainer for advice about how to begin. Under no circumstances should you start a weight program without talking to someone knowledgeable about it first.

A Final Note

Take it from someone who knows: It pays to be in shape. At just about every level of competition, I've played with people with more basketball ability than I have, players who were better shooters, dribblers, and passers. But I've always been able to hold my own because of one simple fact—I could run. I worked hard and got into good condition, and it paid off.

Even if you can't sink a 20-footer or put on a dazzling dribbling exhibition, you'll find a spot on your team if you keep on running and jumping, starting and stopping, when everyone else is dragging. Ball skills are critical, no question about it. But being in top shape can make up for an awful lot of deficiencies.

Work on those exercises I've outlined above. The time commitment doesn't add up to more than a few hours a week, and the benefits will last all season.

Chapter Four

Footwork—The Foundation of Good Basketball

Good basketball begins with good footwork. Basketball is a game of angles, sharp cuts, and quick starts and stops. All the basic skills we'll be talking about in this book spring from your ability to move quickly and sharply, with maximum control and minimum wasted motion. Beating an opponent with the dribble, getting good rebounding position, getting open for a shot, cutting to the basket, playing tough defense—each of these basketball basics demands good footwork.

Being Ready to Move

Since basketball places such a premium on quickness, you've got to be able to move at an instant's notice, and the way to do that is to maintain a *ready* position. Keep your knees flexed, your weight distributed evenly on the balls of your feet, your center of gravity low, and your feet spread comfortably apart.

Whether you're on offense, defense, or going to the boards, this stance will increase your quickness tremendously. With your knees bent and your body well balanced, you can cut, sprint, react—all the moves you must continually make on the court—much faster than when your knees are locked, when you're bending at the waist, or when your movement is uncontrolled.

Think of the stance an animal takes when it's alarmed or on the alert. Immediately it coils into a crouching position, bracing to move and react instantaneously to danger. On the court you want to be able to do the same thing, whether to beat an opponent or to stop her.

Prove to yourself the value of the flexed-kneed stance the next time you're on the court. Toss a ball 15 feet away or so, and first make a cut from a straight-legged position. Feel how long it takes you to react and hit full speed. Then try it with your knees bent. You're moving instantly because your legs are set to go. Every moment is critical in basketball; each fraction of a second you cut off the time it takes you to move or react increases your chances of getting free for a pass, beating your opponent on a drive, stopping her from getting past you when she has the ball, keeping her away from the boards.

Maintain the ready, flexed-kneed position at all times. Being poised to move makes all the difference.

Avoiding the Circle Routes

Think for a moment about a softball player running around the bases. As she approaches each bag, she tries to cut it as tightly as possible. Doing this reduces the distance she has to run. She knows that failing to make good, tight turns will slow her down because she'll wind up running in a looping path that's much less direct.

Smart basketball players try to do the same thing. Concentrate on mak-

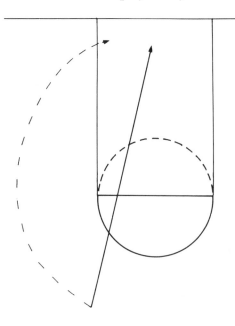

Fig. 4–1 Avoid "great circle routes" on the court. A direct line (as shown) is the shortest and fastest path to your destination.

ing your court moves economical. Make sharp cuts. Run in straight lines. Avoid the great circle routes to your destination; they're wasted motion and make things easier for the defense because they take you out of the play. The shortest distance between two points is a straight line—that's the route you want to take.

Stopping

Quick starts are important, but so are quick, controlled stops. Many inexperienced players, after sprinting all out or shuffling quickly, become off-balanced when they try to stop. Their body weight gets too far forward or to the side, and those few out-of-control moments can take them right out of the play. No matter how fast you run, it won't do you a lot of good on the court if you aren't balanced when you stop.

Your aim is to be under control at all times, and learning the proper ways to stop will help you achieve this. There are two basic stops used in basketball: the jump stop and the stride, or two-step, stop.

The Jump Stop

In the jump stop you break your momentum by landing with both feet simultaneously, almost as if you were jumping to your landing point. This offers several important advantages. One, it allows you to use either foot as a pivot (see Fig. 4–2), thus increasing your freedom of movement. Two, it breaks your forward momentum, leaving you well balanced. And three, it gives you a good, steady base for your shot. It's particularly effective close to the basket and on the fast break, since it allows you to stop and go up for a shot quickly.

To execute the jump stop properly, plant both feet at the same time, pulling your weight back slightly and making sure to flex the knees as you land. This helps cushion the impact and improve body control. The jump stop doesn't actually involve a jump; you're off the ground a small distance, but you're not taking a flying leap before landing. It may take some practice for you to feel comfortable jump stopping, but keep at it. It's a great way to stop quickly and in a way that leaves you ready for whatever comes next. Remember to keep your knees bent when jump stopping. If you try it with straight knees, more than likely you'll keel right over. Plant your feet firmly, with the knees flexed, and you'll find you can stop your forward momentum on a dime.

Fig. 4–2 To execute the jump stop, plant both feet simultaneously, keeping the knees flexed for good balance and readiness. The jump stop allows you to use either foot as your pivot foot, and helps generate upward momentum for your shot.

The Two-Step, or Stride, Stop

Most of us have used the two-step, or stride, stop from the time we began playing basketball. It involves simply putting down one foot after the other, again bending the knees to keep your momentum from carrying you off balance. The stride stop can be executed from a higher rate of speed than the jump stop, so it's good to use in the open court or when you're moving quickly on the perimeter. The disadvantage with this stop is that you can pivot only on the last foot to make contact with the floor after you receive the ball or pick up the dribble. If you use the other foot, it's a traveling violation, and a turnover.

Work on both of these stops, so you're able to apply the brakes quickly and smoothly, under control and with no wasted motion. Remember, economy of movement is what you're after on the court. Why take three steps to stop when you can do it in one?

Fig. 4–3 On the stride stop, you put your feet down one after the other. Here, too, keep the knees bent.

Pivoting

When you have the ball, the rules permit you to step in any direction with one foot as long as the other, called the pivot foot, is held in the same position. This freedom allows you to execute fakes, turn to face the basket, pivot away from defensive pressure, use your body to protect the ball, or improve a passing angle to a teammate.

Keep these simple guidelines in mind when pivoting:
• You cannot change your pivot foot. Once you've begun pivoting on one foot, it's a violation to pick up that foot and begin pivoting on the other.
• Use the ball of your foot when pivoting. This allows for maximum range of movement, enabling you to move freely in whatever direction is necessary. Stay off your heel! Pivoting on your heel is a sure way to get your legs all twisted up and to invite traveling violations, because it makes it almost impossible to keep your foot stationary. As always, be sure to maintain your bent-knee "ready" stance for maximum balance and agility.

Forward Pivots and Reverse Pivots

It's important to learn to pivot comfortably in both directions. These moves are called the forward pivot (when your chest leads the way) and the reverse pivot (when your rear end leads the way). You'll use each of these moves dozens of times in every game, with and without the ball. Pivots are used to change direction, establish position, square up to the basket, box out, and in lots of other ways. In every instance, whether executing the forward or reverse pivot, you should pivot on the ball of your foot and with your knees bent.

Fig. 4–4 The chest leads the way when making a forward pivot *(right)*.

The rear end leads when making a reverse pivot *(far right)*.

Change of Direction

We've talked about how basketball is a game of angles, not circles. On offense and defense (and in transition from one to the other), you have to change directions constantly, and how well you do this has a lot to do with how well you play the game.

The key is to cut at a good, sharp angle. A lazy cut, one where you don't make a distinct change of direction, is not much better than no cut at all. To change direction properly, allow these guidelines:
- Run, as always, with your knees flexed. Being in the ready position shortens the time necessary to make the change.
- Plant your outside foot firmly to stop your momentum.
- Rotate your hips in the direction you want to go, shift your weight, push off with your planted foot, and pick up the pace with an explosive start.

Say you want to make a sharp change of direction to the left to receive a pass. Running with your knees well bent, plant your right foot, rotate the hips quickly to the left, push off hard on the right foot and accelerate to full speed. When you change direction this way, you can make turns quickly and eliminate wasted motion.

Footwork Drills

Start and Stop

Measure a distance about the length of a court and mark it off into thirds. Sprint the first third and execute a jump stop. Do the same at the next two markings. On the way back, make stride stops. Rest and repeat.

Diagonal Run

On a court or other wide, flat area of about the same length, sprint diagonally about 10 yards, make a sharp cut, then sprint another 10 yards and change direction again. Execute one more sprint and change of direction. Rest, and repeat on the way back.

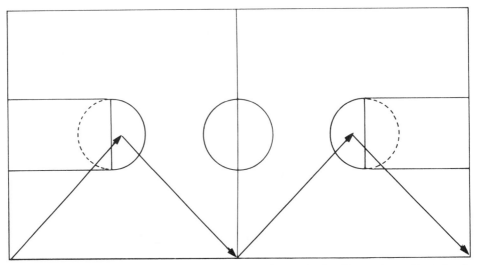

Fig. 4–5 Concentrate on making sharp stops and turns in the diagonal run. Push hard off the foot opposite to where you want to go, rotating the hips and staying in a bent-knee position. After pivoting, explode with a hard first step.

Pivot Drill

Holding the ball and using your right foot as the pivot foot, pivot in different directions, making sure to move only on the ball of your foot. Make a forward pivot, then come back with a reverse pivot. Change to the left foot as your pivot foot and repeat the exercise, getting yourself accustomed to the freedom of movement a simple pivot allows you.

Run and Pivot

Measure a distance of about ten yards. Sprint to the line, make a jump stop and execute a reverse pivot with your left foot as the pivot foot. Sprint back and repeat the reverse pivot off the left foot. Start again, run to the line, but this time make a forward pivot off the left foot at both stops. Rest, and repeat the exercise with the right foot as your pivot, first making two reverse pivots, then two forward pivots.

A Final Thought

Footwork is one of the most neglected phases of basketball instruction. Many coaches and players are so intent on developing the ball skills—shooting, passing, dribbling—that they fail to appreciate the importance of footwork. But without proper footwork even the most polished ball skills will be of limited value.

The feet are the foundation of the body, and footwork is the foundation of good basketball. It's what allows you to put your other skills to their best use. Pay attention to your footwork. Work on making sharp cuts, running at angles and not circles. Make good, hard stops and quick changes of direction. Learn to pivot smoothly and comfortably—off both feet and in both directions. Strive to make your court movements as efficient as possible.

Quickness and control are what you're after in basketball, and that's why, above all, you have to remember to keep your knees flexed and your weight evenly distributed on the balls of your feet. Nothing on the court should be done standing up straight. Be ready and stay ready. If you do, you won't just be able to keep up with the pace . . . you may be setting it.

Chapter Five

Your Best Shot

Every basketball game is won by the team that scores the most points. Think shooting's important? You bet it is.

Shooting is the most glamorous part of basketball. No matter the playing level, you'll get the glory if you can put the ball in the hoop. It's the easiest skill to appreciate. A lot of fans may not notice whether you're adept at boxing out or making a bounce pass. But pump in five jumpers in a row and you'll have the place buzzing.

That's why being a good shooter can take you a long way. I've seen players with glaring weaknesses in other facets of the game who guaranteed themselves playing time simply because they were so good at scoring. That's not the type of player *you* want to be, because the best players are those with the all-around skills. But as a coach, I know shooting ability is tough to overlook. In soccer they use the term "finisher" to describe a goal scorer, because he or she is capable of finishing the play by putting the ball behind the goalkeeper. The term applies to basketball as well. If you can finish your team's offensive sequence, you will be a valuable asset indeed.

A Born Shooter?

Often basketball people talk about a player as a "great natural shooter." While it's true that some players have better hand-eye coordination and seem to have a naturally soft touch, the description is not accurate. Every great shooter I've known has achieved that skill by taking hundreds and hundreds of shots every day. Practice may not make perfect, but it certainly pushes you in that direction. So don't put too much stock in the natural-shooter talk. If you want to be a good shooter, you have to practice shooting, and that's all there is to it.

Triple-Threat Position

You've received the ball from a teammate. The first thing you should do is square up, positioning yourself so you're facing the basket. Having done that, you're now in what's known as triple-threat position, meaning you have the option of shooting, passing, or dribbling. With all these options, you give the defensive player a lot to think about. How should she play you? Should she lay off? If she does, you may get an uncontested shot, or be able to make an easy pass to a teammate. Should she guard you closely? Maybe, but then you may be able to drive right around her and get an easy shot at the basket. The defender has to be on the lookout for all three options, and that makes her job much more difficult. Which is precisely what you want when you're on offense.

Shooting is always the first choice, so you look for an opportunity. Nobody is in better shooting position and you're not being closely guarded. You elect to put it up. Let's look at how to give yourself the best shot at scoring.

Fig. 5–1 Triple-threat position. The player is ready—and in good position—to shoot, pass, or dribble.

Balance

Good shooting begins with good body balance. Your weight should be evenly distributed, on the balls of your feet. Don't lean backward or forward. Many young players, wanting to get something extra on the ball, lean forward and wind up drifting in toward the basket as they shoot, which creates two problems. One, it throws the shot off because of the forward momentum, and two, it makes you prone to committing an offensive foul by charging into a defender.

Your feet should be staggered (with the foot on the side of your shooting hand a few inches ahead of its mate) and roughly shoulder-width apart. Also be sure to keep your knees bent. This is very important. Bent knees improve your balance and body control, and supply a great deal of the power required to get the ball up to the basket. Try shooting a 15-foot shot stiff-legged, with no bend. It's not easy, is it? If you don't flex the knees you'll wind up shooting with only your arms, which will greatly reduce your accuracy. "Arm" shooters tend to hoist the ball, lacking the necessary soft touch.

Keeping Your Head Still

The position of your head is another key element to good balance. If it's moving around or off to the side when you're trying to shoot, your body will be off balance, and the shot, more than likely, will be off target. So work on keeping your head straight up and still when you're shooting. Moving it is only wasted motion, and that's something you want to eliminate completely in shooting. Keep it simple. Don't make *any* move, whether it's with your head, arms, or legs, that isn't contributing positively to your shooting motion. Every extraneous movement is another chance for something to get fouled up.

Minding Your Elbow

If you don't have a basketball at your side, now would be a good time to go get one. Having a ball will help you get a feel for what I'm talking about as we go along.

Elbow position may be the single most important ingredient in good shooting. The slightest wandering of the elbow leads to inconsistent shooting, no matter what else you do right. Here's where it should be:
•Directly under the ball, in line with the basket and bent in an L position.
•In a straight line with your foot, knee, hip, and shooting hand. Don't let your elbow drift out away from your body, a common mistake that throws the shot off. It's the same as when you're throwing a dart; if the elbow is out to the right (for a right-hander), the dart (or ball) will go right. If the elbow's aligned properly, it'll go straight.

Fig. 5–2 Keep your elbow directly under the ball when shooting, making sure it's lined up with your foot, knee, and hip, as the photograph shows. If you let the elbow drift outward, your shooting won't be consistent.

Improving Your Ball Control

You need a soft touch to be a good shooter. You get it by controlling the ball with the pads of your fingers. The palm is your arch enemy in shooting. If you let the ball sit in your palm, you lose the sensitivity needed to shoot well. Look at Fig. 5–3. Notice the sliver of space between the shooter's hand and the ball; that's how you know you're holding the ball properly. If you don't have that space, you're going to have less control, and you're going to score fewer points.

Fingers should be slightly cupped, comfortably spread, holding the ball firmly but not tensely. The shooting hand should be in the middle of the ball. To check for the right position, find the valve on the ball and place your hand so the valve is directly between the "V" formed by your index and middle fingers. Your off hand (the one you're not shooting with) is directly on the side of the ball, making it easier to control and shoot straight.

Fig. 5–3 Good shooting requires a good touch. Keep the ball on the pads of the fingers with the hand slightly cupped. There will be a sliver of air between your palm and the ball when you're holding it properly.

Releasing the Ball

The elbow acts as a hinge when you shoot a basketball. You release the ball by lifting your arm, springing your forearm forward, and snapping the wrist. Don't push the ball; it's hard to have any kind of touch shooting that way.

As the ball leaves your hand, it should roll off your fingertips with a smooth, even backspin. If the spin is to the side, you know your hand placement is wrong. Pay close attention to the alignment we discussed: The elbow should be lined up with your foot, knee, and hip. And remember to maintain the elbow in that L position, which will ensure that you don't release the shot too low. Some beginning players feel more comfortable shooting from near their chest, but avoid getting into this habit. It's not good form, and it makes your shot much easier to block.

Fig. 5–4 Proper hand placement on the ball. Your shooting hand should be directly behind the ball, fingers comfortably spread, with the "V" formed by your forefinger and middle finger centered on the ball. Your off hand is on the side, helping to guide the ball in the direction you want.

Why Arc Is Important

You have greater margin for error when you shoot the ball high than when you shoot it as a low line drive. That's why you want to arch your shots so they go well over the rim, whether you're shooting for the backboard or straight for the basket. As the ball descends, it has more rim to land in. (In fact, if you stood directly over the rim, you could fit two basketballs side by side inside the hoop.) A high-arching shot is also much softer, so you'll increase the chances that your shot, if not perfect, will roll off the rim and still drop through. Line-drive shots have to be nearly perfect to score.

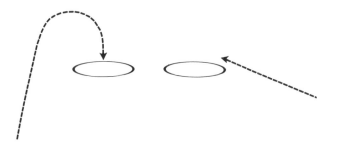

Fig. 5–5 It's basic physics: You have more of the basket exposed to the ball when you shoot with a high arc.

Follow-Through

One of the most neglected aspects of shooting is the follow-through, and that's unfortunate, because a good finish to the shot is almost as important as the shot itself. The follow-through is crucial to having a soft touch. If you snap your hand downward after shooting, or if you pull it back almost as if you'd touched a hot stove, the ball tends to hit the rim harder, making it bounce away rather than drop. You lose a feel for the shot, as well as the backspin that occurs naturally when the ball rolls off the fingertips.

For a good follow-through, keep your hands up after the shot, your arms fully extended, and pretend you're looping the index and middle fingers of your shooting hand just over the front edge of the rim. Your wrist should be loose and flexed forward for a nice fluid finish to your shot. In this way your entire motion is flowing forward, as if it were guiding the flight of the ball. A good follow-through also lets you check your shooting technique. If the shooting hand is turned inward or outward, you know you've released the ball with a twist—extra motion that you don't want. Get in the habit of looking at your shooting hand after the shot is released. If you're not shooting as well as you'd like, the position of the hand may tell you why.

Eyes on the Hoop

Keep your eyes on the basket at all times when shooting, from the moment you're preparing to shoot right to the end of your follow-through. Don't follow the flight of the ball and don't watch the defender's hand. These are common mistakes, and big ones. There's no way you can shoot well if you're not concentrating on your target. Where precisely to focus the eyes depends on where you're shooting from. On a bank shot, your eyes should be riveted to the area of the board you want to hit. For straight-on shots, my suggestion is to focus on a spot just past the front edge of the rim. Concentrate on shooting the ball just barely up and over that edge. That'll give you some leeway if your shot is long. Some coaches advise players to look at the back part of the rim, and shoot a little shorter. It's six one way, a half-dozen the other. I prefer the front because it's closer, more clearly in view, and because I think concentrating on just slipping the ball up and over that edge encourages a softer shot. In any case, pick your spot and focus on it constantly and consistently, every time you shoot.

Specific Shots

The shooting guidelines we've discussed apply to a variety of shots. Now let's look at the most common of them, and how to get the best possible results.

The Lay-Up

The lay-up, a shot taken using the backboard in close to the basket, is the most basic shot in basketball. It's the first one you should master.

Let's assume you're right-handed. Stand to the right of the basket, about two feet from the hoop. With your left foot planted, bring up your right knee as shown and shoot the ball off the backboard. The leg movement may feel awkward at first, but keep at it. Using this footwork helps get the ball up to the basket, allows you to release the ball at a higher point, and is essential when taking a lay-up on the move because it allows you to shoot with great control.

Once you feel comfortable taking the shot from there, back up a few feet. Now (still on the right of the basket), take one dribble (with your right hand; away from the defense), plant your left foot, bring up your right knee and shoot for the board, just as you did before. Keep backing up as you get used to shooting from each stop. Don't worry too much about speed when you're first learning the lay-up. Just work on keeping your body well balanced and in control, planting your left foot, coordinating the knee and shooting motions. (On the left side of the basket, it's the right foot that's planted and the left leg that's brought up.) Whether you're left- or right-handed, you must learn to shoot the lay-up with either hand.

A few other important things to keep in mind when shooting a lay-up:
- Aim high on the board. Your lay-up should hit the backboard at least a foot over the rim. This arc will improve your chance of making the shot.
- Don't get too far under the hoop before you shoot. A common problem for beginners is taking an extra dribble and getting almost directly beneath the basket—not a good shooting angle. Plant your opposite foot and go up for your lay-up when you're still a few feet out from the basket.
- Until you're set to shoot, keep the ball just outside the hip that is away from the basket. This protects the ball from defenders and makes it easy

Fig. 5–6 Taking a right-handed lay-up. Plant your left foot, bring your right leg up and jump straight up toward the basket. Make sure the jump is vertical. Jumping forward will throw off the shot.

to get the ball up into shooting position.

- Go up straight. The biggest flaw of all among inexperienced lay-up shooters is attempting the shot with a flying forward leap, resulting in out-of-control shots, horrible shooting percentages, and lots of headaches for coaches. The lay-up isn't a broad jump. Get into the habit of driving hard to the basket, but then pulling up and going up straight toward the basket; in other words, with upward momentum and not forward momentum.
- Concentrate on the board. Pick out the spot on the backboard you want to hit and keep your eyes fixed on it throughout the shooting motion. Of course, you'll be able to do this only if you've been working on dribbling with your head up.
- Keep your nonshooting hand on the ball until the moment you release the shot. Taking it off too soon makes it difficult to control the ball.
- Use the backboard on all close shots, no matter what angle you're taking them from. The only exception is when you're shooting from the baseline and there is no board to shoot for.

As you get more proficient at the lay-up, work on getting high off the ground with your push-off step, and in going up hard toward the basket. Few lay-ups in games will be uncontested; by taking yours with authority, you'll discourage most defenders from stopping you, or if they try, increase the likelihood you'll be fouled. Go up for the lay-up with confidence. Jump high, power your way toward the hoop, and think of it as a sure two points. And if there's contact, continue through with your shot in spite of it. The two points might wind up being three if you're fouled.

Having a good, strong lay-up is a must for every player. It's a frequently taken shot—one you've got to be able to make a high percentage of the time in order to play successfully.

The Jump Shot

The jump shot has made up for lost time. Though it didn't become widespread until the 1950s, it has emerged as the most popular and important offensive weapon in basketball.

As the name suggests, a jump shot (or jumper, as it's often called) is a shot released after you jump—ideally, at the peak of your jump—making it difficult to block. But don't worry too much in the beginning about shooting at the top of your jump. I've worked with a number of young players who've gotten the mechanics of their shot all twisted up by thinking too much about the jumping and not enough about the shooting. A couple of extra inches on your jump is not worth that. Master the shot first, then try to coordinate the jump with it later.

More than with any other shot, the legs are critical to your being a good jump shooter. Why? Because jumpers often are taken from 15 or 20 feet out, and you need the power of the legs to get the ball to the basket, as well as up and over your defender. In close you can get by without much

Fig. 5–7 When taking a jump shot, strive for a smooth, flowing motion and consistency of form. It should feel the same every time. Notice how the legs are bent and the foot on the side of the shooting hand is slightly forward *(top left and right)*. Jump straight up and release the ball on a soft, arching path to the basket *(bottom left)*. Follow through *(bottom right)* by keeping your hands up as shown, as though you're hooking the fingers of your shooting hand just over the front edge of the rim.

bend in the knees by relying on upper-body strength, but shooting a jumper that way will result in a push more than a shot. You can't get either distance or control by pushing the ball.

Important points to keep in mind regarding jump shooting include:

• Square your shoulders to the basket. The center of your body should be perpendicular to the spot you're shooting for. Don't shoot from the side or off your shoulder. By facing the basket, you improve your sight line and invite a smooth, straight release on your shot.

• Use a one-step motion. A jump shot should be a smooth, flowing shot in which all the movements are well-coordinated. As you go up, the power from your flexed knees is smoothly transferred to a smooth, effortless release. It'll take a little time to get this flowing motion down, but it's time well spent. A jerky shooting motion disrupts your rhythm—and will do bad things to your shooting percentage.

• Go up straight. Don't drift when you go up for a jumper. You should land *slightly* ahead of the spot where you left your feet. Fading away will make it difficult to reach the basket, and falling forward will usually make the shot too strong. If you can't reach the basket without jumping forward, you're shooting from too far out.

• Don't forget the follow-through. We've talked about it already, but it's worth a reminder here, because the follow-through is more important on a jumper than any other shot. It's critical that you keep your hand up so the shot lands softly on the rim and that all your movement is flowing in the same, forward direction.

The Bank Shot

The backboard is often the shooter's best friend. It gives you more margin for error on the shot than the rim does. Get in the habit of using it when you're in a backboard spot; as a rule, that means when you're anywhere

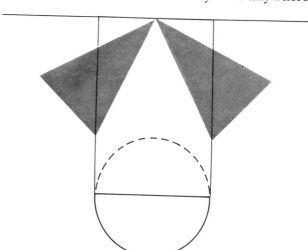

Fig. 5–8 When in the shaded areas, you should generally shoot for the backboard instead of the rim.

in close or when you're at about a 45-degree angle to the basket. Remember to concentrate on the spot you want to hit and to shoot the ball with a nice, soft arch, giving you more rim to hit when the ball skips off the board. The farther out you're shooting, the higher on the board you should aim.

The Free Throw

As both a player and a coach, I've been on the short end of games in which the failure to make free throws, or foul shots, was the cause of defeat. Few things in basketball are as frustrating as outplaying your opponent and scoring more field goals, only to lose because you sank 5 of 14 from the line and they went 16 for 20. Making free throws is often the decisive factor in close games . . . especially down the stretch or when playoff time rolls around.

Proper foul-shooting form is the same as with other shots. Stand with your feet in a staggered position (for right-handers, the right foot slightly ahead of the left), about shoulder-width apart. The knees, as always, are flexed. Here are some other foul-shooting hints:

•Take a few deep breaths before shooting. This helps relax you, and you've got to be relaxed when you're taking any shot.

•Get comfortable. Bounce the ball, tug at your jersey, bend your knees—do whatever makes you feel comfortable at the line. There's no need to rush; you have a full ten seconds to get the ball off after the official gives it to you. Try to develop a routine to go through every time you take a free throw. The idea is to make the whole process as familiar as possible, so the shooting motion will come naturally to you, even in a pressured game situation.

•Use your legs! They make it much easier to get the ball to the hoop with a smooth, flowing shooting motion—and without jumping, which you want to avoid if you possibly can when free-throw shooting; this is just unnecessary motion that complicates the shot. (I know this is difficult for many smaller and/or younger players, even with the knees flexed, so if you need to jump, do so to avoid throwing off your shot by using too much arm.)

•Create some kind of pressure when practicing free throws. Have a contest if you're shooting with another player. If you're practicing alone, set different goals. Maybe one time you'll keep shooting until you make five in a row. Or perhaps you'll stick with it until you make 15 out of 25. Work on injecting an element of pressure into your free-throw practice sessions. It'll help a lot when it comes time to take them under the pressure of games.

•Practice free throws when you're tired, such as after running sprints or at the end of practice. It's not much use being completely well-rested when practicing free throws because you'll almost never be shooting them under such conditions in a game.

•Your free-throw shooting motion should be the same as your regular shot.

Just remember to take full advantage of the luxury of not having a defender to contend with. Take your time, get set and make yourself comfortable. It's just you and the basket.

What's a Good Shot for You?

Often you'll hear a coach criticize a player for poor shot selection. What determines whether a shot is a good or bad choice? It depends on the player and the circumstances under which the shot is taken. If you're a six-foot center who is rarely more than a few feet from the basket and you try an 18-footer, that's a poor shot to take, regardless of the results. The same shot for a point guard, however, may be just fine, provided she is generally accurate from that range. Timing is critical, too. If the other team has scored 15 straight points, the last thing you want to do is come down fast and throw up a 15-footer right away, no matter how good a shooter you are. Under such circumstances, your aim is to slow down the game's tempo, take the edge off their momentum and work the ball around to force them to play defense.

As a player, it's vital to know what shots you should and shouldn't be taking. You hurt yourself and your team if you don't—not just by hastily firing up low-percentage shots, but also by not taking shots you should. I coached a player once who practically never looked to the basket. She had little confidence in scoring and was happy to leave the shooting to others. But what she had to learn was that her unselfishness was hurting the team, because smart defenses quickly realized they could just about ignore her altogether.

If you're not sure about what shots you should be looking for, ask your coach. She'll let you know when and where she wants you to be looking to shoot. To be a complete player, you must be willing and able to put the ball up.

Hints for Better Shooting

•Be patient. Even the best shooters have a tough time making over 50 percent of their shots. Don't get discouraged if you're not pouring in the points. Keep setting new goals, and strive for improvement every day.
•Don't waste practice time. Practice the shots you'll most likely be taking in a game. Shooting running one-handers from midcourt can be fun, but it's not going to do much to improve your shooting.
•Start close to the basket and work your way out. No sense trying to run a marathon before you can run a mile, right? Begin practicing your shooting technique with five- and six-foot shots. Shoot for touch first and worry about range later. Get comfortable taking shots from all spots on the court, then gradually work your way out, being conscious of maintaining the same proper form.
•Strive for consistency of form. After you get the hang of proper shooting

technique, every shot should begin to feel the same. The more you practice, the more natural your shot will feel. Keep at it so you're able to feel when you've done something wrong—not followed through properly, not used enough leg in the shot, let your elbow stray from your body, whatever. The more tuned in you are to the right way, the less chance there will be that you'll lapse into the wrong way.

• Stay relaxed. Tension can destroy the soft touch needed to shoot well. Your body, from feet to fingertips, should feel loose and fluid throughout your shooting motion.

• Just about everybody has favorite and not-so-favorite shooting spots. Keep track of the spots where you're having trouble, and put in extra practice time at them.

• Build your confidence. I can't say I know why, but it sure seems to be true that if you expect to get good results, you will. Believe in yourself and your ability to make a shot. Go up with confidence. Think positively. Tell yourself, "I'm going to put this ball in the hoop."

Shooting Drills

On-Your-Back Drill

This is a good way to develop shooting form. After recruiting someone to retrieve the ball, lie flat on the floor and hold the ball in shooting posi-

Fig. 5–9 On-your-back drill. Lying flat on your back with a spotter standing as shown, shoot the ball directly upward, being careful to maintain good form. If you're shooting properly, the ball will fall right back into your hands.

tion: elbow in, ball on the pads of your fingers, off hand on the side of the ball, and the ball above your shoulder, aligned with your foot, knee, and hip. Shoot the ball as you would at the basket, snapping your wrists and rolling it off your fingertips so it will come back down to your hands. If it does, then you've got the right shooting form. If it doesn't, you're doing something wrong; go back to the basics and find out what's off. Repeat the exercise until the ball has come back to you 10 times.

Line Drill

Another good way to polish your shooting technique. Put a piece of tape on the floor between you and another player, who's about ten feet away. With a regular, high-arching shooting motion, practice "shooting" the ball back and forth to each other, trying to make the ball land on the tape. Keep at it until each of you has hit the tape 10 times. Like the prior drill, this will show you very clearly if you're doing things correctly. If the ball's not hitting the line, your alignment is off somewhat.

Touch Drill

Stand at the side of the basket, four feet from the hoop. Concentrate on your form and getting a good soft feel for the ball. Bend your knees, and as you spring up to release the shot with a snap of your wrist, extend your arm and follow through, keeping your hand up until the ball drops through the net. (Got to think positively, remember?) Feel the ball roll off your fingertips and check for the desired backspin. Take 10 shots from each of the five shooting positions shown (shots 2 and 4 should be bank shots), maintaining sound form. Try not to touch the rim with the ball on this drill. Concentrate on making every shot perfect, getting the ball well up and over the rim so it will fall cleanly through the iron.

Intensity Lay-Up

The shooter (A) starts with the ball near the foul line as shown in Fig. 5–10. Player A sends a crisp chest pass to Player B, fakes away from the ball, then cuts sharply to the basket. Player B returns the pass at the point shown, roughly six feet out. Player A goes in for a lay-up, dribbling as needed, depending on where she receives the ball. She gets her own rebound, dribbles back to the foul line and repeats the drill. Do as many lay-ups as you can in 30 seconds, then repeat the drill on the other side of the lane. Dribble and shoot with the right hand on the right side, left hand on the left.

Inside the Lane

Set up a partner with the ball about 15 feet out on the wing. Start on the far side of the lane, come hard toward the ball and have her throw a bounce pass to you when you reach the edge of the lane nearest her. As you catch it, jump stop and forward pivot on your inside foot, square your

Fig. 5–10 Intensity lay-up. Pass the ball to the wing *(top),* fake away, then cut hard to the basket *(center).* After your teammate makes a bounce pass back to you, go up strongly for the lay-up *(bottom),* taking a dribble if you're too far away to go up without one.

shoulders to the basket by bringing your outside foot around and go up for the shot, straight and strong. Follow your shot, return the ball to the partner, and repeat until you've taken 10 shots. Switch roles, then repeat the drill on the other side of the court. This drill hones two important skills—stopping quickly and getting a shot off after a quick movement.

Around the World

Set up five spots along an imaginary semicircle, each about 12 feet from the basket. Take ten shots from each spot, and keep track of your record.

If another player is available, you can also play a two-person version of Around the World. The spots remain the same, but the object here is to be the first player to go "around the world" twice—that is, back and forth over the five spots two times (twenty spots in all). The rules are simple. If you make a shot, you move to the next spot and continue until you miss. After a miss, you have two choices: You can stay at that spot and let the other player begin her turn, or you can "risk," meaning take another shot from the spot you missed from. If you make it, you continue on to the next location. But if you miss, it's all the way back to the beginning. This game is a lot of fun, and gives you some practice in shooting under pressure.

Cut and Stop

Similar to the Intensity Lay-Up Drill, except here the shooter pulls up for a ten-foot shot. Player A passes to B, then cuts sharply to the basket. At the spot shown, Player B feeds Player A with a pass, and A goes up for a jump shot.

Remember to jump stop and plant your feet solidly before going up for your shot; that's the whole secret to doing this drill right and learning to shoot off a cut. Square your shoulders to the basket and go up straight. If you don't go straight, the ball won't either.

Rapid Fire

You'll need to recruit a rebounder for this drill, which is a good way to work on getting your shot off quickly. Set up about 10 feet out. Take a shot, get a pass from the rebounder, and go up again, shooting as quickly as you can without sacrificing good form. Take ten shots from a spot, then switch, so you rebound and feed her. Continue switching until each of you has taken ten shots from five different spots.

Thirty-Second Drill

Get someone to rebound and set up about 15 feet out. Take as many shots as you can in 30 seconds, trying to shoot 10 shots from five different spots. Concentrate on releasing the ball quickly while maintaining sound technique. Step into the ball as the rebounder passes it to you so you're prepared to shoot the moment you get it. Keep track of the number of shots taken and the number of shots made. They'll both increase the more you work on this drill. Switch with the rebounder after your 30 seconds are up.

Be Creative

One great thing about shooting is that you can do it anytime and just about anywhere. You don't need a coach or teammate. All you need is the ball and a rim. Another great thing about it is that you're limited only by your imagination.

There are only so many clever ways you can practice dribbling or rebounding; not so with shooting practice. Make up games that'll stimulate your interest; the more fun practice is, the more you'll do it, and the better shooter you'll become. Here's a brief sampler of possible games:

• Beat the Clock. Keep track of time—30 to 60 seconds is a good range— and count how many baskets you make from one shooting spot. Record the results, and move around to different spots.

• The Buzzer Game. Five . . . four . . . three . . . two . . . Pretend the clock is winding down as you shoot, as though the outcome of the game depended on your shot.

• Station to Station. Designate various shooting stations on the court, and set goals to meet before you move on to the next spot. You might set a flat number of baskets, say 10, as your goal, or you might make it 10 of 20, and stay put until you hit that percentage. Or if you lean toward perfectionism, make yourself hit five in a row before moving along.

• Mix it up. Work on other areas of your game while working on your shooting. Take a shot, rebound it, dribble back out, execute a crossover dribble, then pull up and shoot again. Follow your shot, and this time shoot after a jab step or change-of-pace dribble (we'll look at the best way to execute these moves in chapter 8). Keep mixing things up. Practice making all your moves going both ways and taking shots after cutting in different directions.

Whether you make up your own games or follow the drills I've outlined here, the bottom line when it comes to shooting is to get out there and do it. It's the only way to become a good shooter. You'll get results if you follow the fundamentals we've discussed, and the more you shoot, the faster the results will come. Take as many shots as you can every day. Squeeze in 25 before gym class starts. Shoot a quick 50 when you're on a break from your schoolwork. Before long you'll notice the ball is dropping a lot more often, and, who knows, if you keep at it, maybe sometime soon that buzzing from the crowd will be for you.

Chapter Six

Passing—The Heart of the Game

When I'm playing defense, there are some teams I like going against and others I don't. My favorites are teams that come down, make a pass or two, fire up a shot and call it a possession. From the defender's standpoint, what could be nicer? A few seconds of work and your defensive duties are over.

Not so nice is when a team constantly keeps the ball in motion, whipping it around until they get the shot they want. You can never relax against an offense like that, because you never know where the ball will go next.

Stripped to its basics, basketball really is a simple game. The better the shots that you take (ones that are more open and closer to the basket), the better your chances to win. But those shots don't just materialize by themselves. You have to go out and get them. And you do that by making good passes.

Appreciating the Passing Game

Passing at its best is truly an art form. To watch a player like Larry Bird, who passes as though he has two sets of eyes, is to see a master at work. He makes himself an ever-present threat to the defense because he's capable of passing to any teammate on the court at any time. Learning the basics of passing will make you much more of a threat, too. It'll raise the level of your game, and your team's as well, because good passing is like enthusiasm—it's contagious. Not only does this make your team harder to defend against, it's a much more fun way to play because everyone feels like an integral part of the action.

Why is passing so important? Because it's the fastest way to move the ball around the court. It works the defense and creates scoring opportunities. The defense can never rest against a good, crisp passing game.

Dribbling simply can't compare as a way to move the ball. Say you've got the ball and you spot a teammate cutting to the basket. She's open, but that will last only for a moment before someone picks her up or you lose your angle to get the ball to her. If you dribble toward her and then try to pass, the opportunity will be long gone. Advantages in basketball—such as having an open teammate in scoring position—only last for a fleeting moment. Either you pass or the advantage does.

It Takes Two to Pass

Rule no. 1 of the passing game is that a pass is good only if it is caught. Even if you've threaded a behind-the-back bullet right into a teammate's hands, if she's caught off guard and fumbles it, the pass has done your team no good at all. It's as important to learn how to catch a pass as it is to learn how to throw one.

Another key is gaining a sense of where and when you're a likely target for a passer. This depends on two factors—the position of the ball and the position of the defender nearest you. You must be alert to both. Clearly, if you're only eight feet from a teammate and you've got a wide-open lane to the basket, chances are good you'll be getting the ball. But other times it's not so obvious. A teammate may see a passing opportunity that you don't. That's why it's important to follow the ball at all times, and to keep your hands up at waist level so you can catch a pass at split-second notice. Not knowing where the ball is or not being ready to catch it is all it takes for a perfectly good pass to bounce away from you.

Meet the Pass

You're about to receive a pass, but that doesn't mean you should be passive. Don't stand there waiting for the ball to come to you; chances are it never will. You have to "come to the ball," as we coaches like to say. By slightly shortening the distance the ball has to travel, this small effort is often the difference between a completed pass and an intercepted one. It's also a good way to draw a foul on your defender; if you meet the pass and she tries to steal it, the chances are good that she may get a piece of you instead of the ball.

Receiving a Pass

What happens when you drop a ball onto a hard floor? It bounces. What happens when you drop it onto a pillow? The impact is cushioned, and the ball settles softly into place.

The same distinction holds when you're catching a basketball. If your arms and hands are rigid and tense, the ball will bounce away from you. If you keep them loose and give with the pass, it'll settle comfortably and safely into place. Here are some pointers when you're on the receiving end of a pass:

• Give your teammate a good target. As the ball is passed, extend your arms out from your body and hold your hands with the fingertips up. Your thumbs should be pointing toward each other, with your fingers spread comfortably so they'll touch as much of the ball as possible.

• Bend your elbows and give with the ball as it arrives by bringing your hands in toward your body. Pull the ball in close and keep your elbows out so it's well protected.

Fig. 6–1 It's important to be ready to catch a pass. Keep your hands up and thumbs together, with your fingers spread so you have more of your hand to catch the ball with.

- Look the ball into your hands. Most missed passes are fumbled not because of defensive pressure, but because the receiver takes her eye off the ball. Follow the ball right into your hands.
- Do one thing at a time. Basketball is such a fast-paced game that it's easy to get caught up in the action and hurry too much. But haste makes waste— and turnovers. You'll fumble the pass if you try to rush downcourt before having firm possession of the ball.
- Get behind the pass. It's not always possible, but, whenever you can, position your body so it's directly behind the ball. It's like an infielder in baseball. If you move so that you're squarely in line with the ball, you can still play it off your body even if you don't field it cleanly with your hands. Getting behind the pass gives you insurance against losing possession.

Fig. 6–2 Proper hand placement for throwing a pass: Thumbs close together, elbows in, fingers spread comfortably over the ball.

Basic Types of Passes

Different situations call for different passes. Here's a rundown on the most common passes you'll need to make.

The Chest Pass

This is the most common pass in basketball. While it's not difficult to execute, it's a pass many players get lazy with and execute sloppily as a result.

Begin with the ball at chest level, close to your body. Keep the elbows in. Your hands should be up, your fingers spread and your thumbs pointing

Fig. 6–3 The chest pass. Step toward your target *(left)* and snap the ball off quickly by extending your arms. Follow through with palms facing out and thumbs pointing down *(right).*

toward each other, with the ball on the pads of your fingers. Step toward your target, thrust your arms outward, and release the ball with both hands with a quick snap of the wrists. As you release it, shift your weight from the back foot to the front and finish the chest pass with a good follow-through: arms fully extended, thumbs pointing down and palms facing out, as shown. This will give the ball extra zip and accuracy.

Aim for the number on your teammate's jersey. Thrown anyplace else, a snappy chest pass can be difficult to handle. Work on making your chest passes crisp, as they must be in a game. Lazy passes give the defense more time to stay with the ball and greatly increase the chances of an interception.

The Bounce Pass

The bounce pass is a valuable offensive weapon in several specific situations. It's a must when you want to hit a cutting teammate on a fast break, when a defender is standing up and/or waving her arms overhead, when you have to maneuver the ball past a taller player (who will have trouble getting down to deflect it), and in tight spots where a maze of arms and bodies makes a chest pass too risky (as is usually the case in the post area close to the basket).

The bounce pass is similar to the chest pass, except for the direction of the ball and follow-through. Start with the ball near your body, waist high.

Fig. 6–4 Like the chest pass, the bounce pass begins with a step toward the receiver *(left)*. Aiming for a spot two-thirds of the distance to her, snap the ball off crisply and follow through by extending your arms toward the floor *(right)*.

Your hands should be up, slightly cupped, with the fingers spread over the ball and the thumbs close together. Step toward your target, knees flexed, and snap off the pass with an outward thrust of your wrists, following through by extending your hands toward the floor. Aim for a spot on the floor two-thirds of the way between you and your target. The ball should bounce up to your target between the knee and the waist. If it comes up any higher (and it will if you hit the floor halfway between the two of you), the pass will be an easy steal or deflection for the defense. On the other hand, if you bounce it too close to the target, it'll reach her at about calf-level and be nearly impossible to handle cleanly.

Fig. 6–5 Aim for a spot two-thirds of the way between you and your team-mate when making a bounce pass. Bouncing the ball too close to you re-sults in a high pass that's easy to intercept; bouncing it too close to your team-mate makes it too low for her to handle easily.

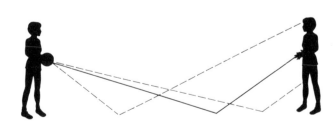

The Baseball Pass

When you want to hit a teammate far upcourt, use the baseball pass. It's not effective in heavy traffic because it takes more time to release than other passes. But for throwing the ball long distances it's definitely the pass of choice.

Take the ball with both hands and pull it back over your throwing shoulder. Place your throwing hand behind the ball, with the off hand slightly lower and in front. Draw the ball back a little more, release your guide hand from the ball and throw it as you would a baseball or softball toward your target, making sure to follow through by bringing your arm down in front of you. It's a good idea to put an arc on the ball so it will carry farther and be easier to catch.

Fig. 6–6 The baseball pass is the best way to advance the ball a long distance. Draw the ball back behind your shoulder *(left)*, then bring your arm forward and release the ball as you would a softball or baseball *(center)*. Follow through to add zip and accuracy to the pass. *(right)*

The Overhead Pass

The overhead pass is recommended when your opponent is short or in a deep crouch; when you're throwing an outlet pass to begin a fast break, when you're making a skip pass against a zone (a skip pass is a pass thrown to a teammate two players away, thus "skipping" over the player in between), or when you want to get the ball to a taller teammate inside. Hold the ball just above the top of your forehead (keep the ball in your sight), with elbows bent, wrists cocked for extra snap, and thumbs close together near the bottom of the ball. Be sure to grasp the ball firmly, with fingers spread. Step forward, shift your weight from back to front and release the ball with a snapping movement of your elbows and wrists, following through with your arms extended—as with a chest pass, only higher.

The degree of "snap" depends on how you're using the pass. To lob it in to the pivot, you want to pass softly, arching it over the defense to your teammate. When attempting a sharper pass, such as to a teammate about ten yards away, the forward snap should continue until your hands are almost parallel to the floor.

Fig. 6–7 The overhead pass. Holding the ball with two hands, pull it back over your head, step toward your receiver *(left),* and release the pass with a forward snapping of the forearms and wrists *(right).* Be careful not bring the ball back so far that you lose sight of it. Use the overhead pass when you are attempting a skip pass, an outlet pass, or trying to lob the ball to the low post.

Helpful Hints for Betting Passing

•Don't telegraph your passes. That's basketball jargon for letting the defense know your intent by looking directly at your target the whole time you're preparing to pass. An alert defensive team will make you pay for every telegraphed pass.

How can you avoid it? Lots of ways. The simplest is by looking away— at another teammate, at the basket, anywhere other than directly at the person you're passing to. Faking is also a good way to avoid telegraphing. It keeps the defense constantly off balance because they can't be sure where you or the ball is going. You might fake a pass to one player, then quickly pivot and pass to another. Or you might fake a bounce pass and then throw an overhead, or just the opposite: pretend you're going over the top with it, then slip it past the stretched-out defender on a bounce. Faking is the best way to counteract a gambling or overplaying defense—a team that's always trying for steals. They're so intent on getting the ball that every little deception puts them out of position, creating openings for attack.

Here are some other passing tips:

•Pass away from the defense. Direct your passes to the side of your team-mate away from the defender. Otherwise you risk an interception.

•Pass crisply. Lazy passes usually don't get there.

•Fingertip touch. Keep your palms off the ball whenever possible. The ball should rest on the pads of the fingers to ensure top accuracy.

•Be very careful when attempting to pass cross-court. It's dangerous trying to throw the ball so far and through so many defenders. Only when a team-mate is wide open, or when you have a clear opening for an overhead skip pass, should you even think about passing cross-court.

•Always pass when a teammate is in a better position to score. It's called hitting the open player, and if you and your team can do it consistently, you're both going to be very successful.

•Don't make automatic passes. Size up the situation before making your pass. It only takes a moment. Check the defense and the positions of your teammates. Quickly scan the court for passing opportunities. Who's open? Can you safely get her the ball? Is anybody cutting to the hoop? What-ever you do, don't force the ball to a teammate just because a planned play calls for the ball to go to her. Starting a play over or going to your next option is a lot better than causing a turnover.

•Acknowledge a good pass. If you get a good pass from a teammate, tell her so. Get in the habit of praising the pass that leads to the basket—called an assist—as much as the basket itself. You couldn't have gotten the points without the pass. Encourage unselfish play at all times. It'll do wonders for your teamwork.

•Don't dribble before every pass. Some players bounce the ball before they do anything else. This accomplishes nothing. It slows the team's flow and ball movement, makes it easier for the defense to stop you, and also may cause you to miss an open teammate. Don't dribble unless you've got a plan in mind.

Passing Drills

Intensity Passing

Stand about three feet from a teammate and snap off chest passes back and forth, concentrating on making them crisp and chest-high. Look the ball into your hands when receiving. Make sure you catch the ball proper-ly. Reel off 10 passes and catches from there, then move back a foot and do 10 more. Finish with another set of 10 from about six feet apart. For maximum benefit, do the sets as fast as you can without getting sloppy, and exaggerate the form and follow-through to ensure that your movements are correct.

This is a valuable drill on several counts. It works on your chest-passing technique, improves the agility of your hands as well as your hand-eye co-ordination, and builds strength in your wrists and forearms.

Defender in the Middle

Two offensive players stand about ten feet apart, with a defender in the middle. The passers then use whatever pass necessary to get the ball past her. If she's waving her arms trying to defend against an overhead pass, bounce-pass the ball by her. If she's low, go over the top. Whenever you're not sure you can pass safely, execute a fake, which will freeze the defender or put her out of position to deflect it. The defender remains in the middle until she touches a pass (she doesn't have to gain possession), and is replaced by whomever threw it.

Passing on the Move

You'll need some space for this one—a driveway, park, or gym. Line up opposite a teammate, about six feet apart. Using one ball, make crisp chest passes back and forth as you run straight ahead for at least thirty yards. Hold the follow-through until your pass is caught, and give your teammate a good target, with your arms extended and hands up. Return to the starting point in the same fashion, making sure you keep a constant distance between you while you're moving. Repeat the exercise using the bounce pass. This drill is very good for improving your catching and passing while on the run, skills that are essential to the game.

Two-Ball Drill

Position yourself about eight feet from a teammate, each of you with a ball. One of you is designated the bounce passer, the other the chest passer. Make your respective passes simultaneously, and make them fast, timing them so they arrive at about the same time. Concentrate on getting them in and out of your hands as quickly as possible. Make fifty passes each, then switch roles—the bounce passer becomes the chest passer, and vice versa. Complete each pass with a good follow-through, and be sure to watch the ball you're receiving all the way into your hands.

A Final Thought

Crisp passing is the heart of offensive basketball. Good passes lead to good catches, which lead to good ball movement, which leads to good shots. And that, as we've seen, can often lead to winning.

Concentrate on your passing game. Catch the ball cleanly. Get rid of it quickly, and make your pass as easy to catch as possible. Get in the habit of faking your passes so the defense is kept off guard. Keep alert and always know where the ball is, so you'll spot defensive weaknesses instantly and see how to improve your passing position. Practice throwing all the passes we've discussed; you'll need them all at some point. The more passes you can execute effectively, the more problems you'll give the defense. They won't know what to expect, which is precisely the position you want to be in. Keep them moving and keep them guessing. Make them work, and make it as hard as you can for them to stop you. Do it with good, sharp passes, the best way to move the ball on the court.

Chapter Seven

Dribbling Under Control

Mastering the art of dribbling is vital to your development as a basketball player. The reason is simple: If you have the ball and you want to move from Point A to Point B, you have to dribble. It's the only legal way to do it. So if you're not an adept dribbler and can't keep the ball under control, you're at a huge disadvantage. You're bound to commit turnovers, have the ball stolen from you and wind up spending a lot more time than you'd like sitting next to your coach.

When—and When Not—to Dribble

Before getting into the specifics of how to dribble, let's look at the dribble as an offensive weapon, including when it should and should not be used. Far too many players (and coaches, too) pay little attention to this aspect of the game, and their performances suffer for it. Even if you're a dribbling expert, if you bounce the ball at the wrong times you're hurting yourself and your team.

The dribble should be used when you want to:
•Get away from a tight area, such as a corner of the court or anywhere the defense is pressuring you, and you don't have an open teammate to pass to.
•Advance the ball on a fast break, again provided there isn't a teammate open farther upcourt.
•Take advantage of a sloughing defense by moving the ball closer to the basket.

• Beat defensive pressure, particularly man-to-man pressure.
• Drive for the basket.
• Improve your passing angle to a teammate, or move closer to her so you can make a shorter, and thus safer, pass.
• Play "keepaway" from your opponents when you want to maintain possession and/or take time off the clock.
• Balance the court when too many players are on one side.

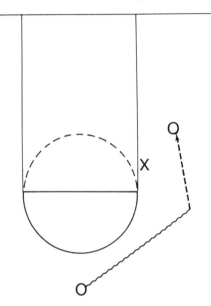

Fig. 7–1 One good use of the dribble is to improve the passing angle to a teammate.

The dribble should *not* be used:
• The moment the ball comes into your hands, before you've sized up the situation.
• When you have an open teammate closer to the basket.
• On a fast break when a teammate is in the open ahead of you.
• Against a zone defense, if you're not penetrating the zone or attempting to exploit a defensive weakness.
• If you are not a ball-handling specialist (that usually means if you're one of the bigger players, such as a center or forward) and you have the ball a long way from the basket. In that case, give the ball up to a guard; it's her job to be a good dribbler.
• Indiscriminately, at any time. If you don't have a plan in mind when you're about to bounce the ball, don't bounce it.

Keep Your Options Open

Let's assume you've just gotten the ball in your offensive area. You move into triple-threat position, so you're ready to shoot, pass or dribble. What you don't want is to become less of a threat by eliminating one of your options. Suppose you're in a game situation. You receive a pass 15 feet from the hoop. Without a thought, the first thing you do is dribble once or twice and then pick up the ball and hold it. Immediately the defensive player is all over you, using her arms and making it difficult for you to shoot or pass.

What has happened? You've wasted your dribble, and the defender, not having to worry about your driving around her now, applies more pressure against the pass and shot. This tendency to dribble automatically the moment you get the ball is probably the most widespread bad habit in basketball. Some players, particularly inexperienced ones, do it out of nervousness. They get the ball, they're a little bit tight, so they bounce it. It's natural. Others do it habitually before they shoot, even though it often gives a defender time to get close enough to contest your shot. Others do it because, well, they got into the habit and never got around to breaking it.

You'll take a giant step toward offensive improvement if you work at not wasting your dribble. Save the dribble for when it counts—and when it can really work to your advantage.

Fig. 7–2 Giving up the dribble reduces your options and allows the defense to apply pressure.

The Dangers of Overdribbling

Another important thing to keep in mind about dribbling is that it's a much slower way to move the ball than passing. I don't care if you're a worldclass sprinter, if you dribble to Point A and I pass to Point A, my pass will get there a lot faster. Since so much of a team's offensive success hinges on quick ball movement, the moral here is: Whenever you have a choice between dribbling and passing to advance the ball, *always pass.*

Slowing down ball movement isn't the only problem caused by too much dribbling. It also tends to make the players who don't have the ball stand around. And once movement away from the ball stops, the offense loses its flow and allows the defense to concern itself only with stopping the player with the ball.

Another hazard in overdribbling is simply that the more you dribble, the better the chance the ball will be stolen or mishandled. Maintaining control of the dribble isn't easy, particularly when you're being closely guarded; using the dribble to excess eventually will get you into trouble.

The key point to remember is that the dribble can be a terrific weapon when used selectively, for a specific offensive purpose such as driving for a lay-up, improving a passing angle, penetrating a zone defense, or moving the ball into a more threatening offensive position. Think before you put the ball to the wood. Soon you'll be able to recognize almost instantly the right and wrong times to dribble.

The Right Way to Dribble

How you dribble depends on the circumstances. There are two basic kinds of dribbles—control and speed. Let's take a look at the best way to perform each.

The Control Dribble

The control dribble is used when you're being closely guarded and you want to keep the ball well-protected and under complete control. It's the dribble you'll use most of the time. The first key here is having a good feel for the ball, and that means handling it with the pads of your fingers. Keep the ball away from your palm. Dribbling with your palm reduces your control and tends to make you slap at the ball.

Spread your fingers loosely over the ball, with your hand slightly cupped. Feeling the ball on the finger pads, push it to the floor with a flexing motion of the wrist. Your elbow is in, close to your body, and your forearm is roughly parallel to the floor. Not much force is necessary to sustain the dribble, so avoid slapping at the ball or pushing it too hard; it'll only make it harder to control.

Keep your legs flexed and your back straight, and dribble the ball no

Fig. 7–3   The control dribble. Note how the knees are flexed for better balance and to keep the dribble low. The head is up, and the off arm is used to protect the ball from the defender.

higher than several inches above your knee, to reduce the time the ball is out of your hand. To shield the ball from the defense, hold the arm you're not dribbling with away from your body. (Be careful, however, not to thrust your arm so far out that it appears you're warding off defenders with it. I've seen a lot of girls whistled for offensive fouls for this, whether there was actual contact or not.) The ball never should be out in front of you, unprotected, because that is just asking the defender to steal it. Keep the ball on your right side when dribbling with your right hand, and the left side when dribbling with your left.

The Speed Dribble

When dribbling on a fast break or downcourt ahead of the field, you want to go fast as you can so the defense can't catch up to you. Since you're in the clear, protecting the ball in such a situation isn't so important. Thus you have the luxury of dribbling the ball higher and pushing the ball farther in front of you. For maximum speed, shift your hand back on the ball so you're able to dribble at an angle well out in front of you (as opposed to the control dribble, where the ball moves straight up and down), and let the ball come up to about waist-level. Just don't let the ball get so high it's out of control. Few things are as exasperating as blowing a wide-open lay-up because the ball bounces away from you.

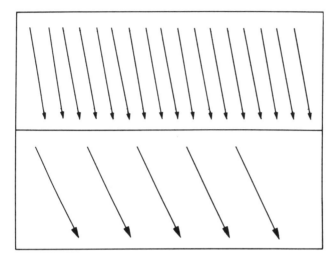

Fig. 7–4 Push the ball well out in front of you when speed dribbling, as shown by the bottom set of arrows. For better ball protection, the control dribble (top) is maintained close to the body and is directed almost straight downward.

Keep Your Head Up

It's very important to keep your head up when you're dribbling. There's a lot happening on the court at any given time. Players, yours and theirs, are constantly moving, and you must know where they are. You may be dribbling downcourt, for example, when a teammate is open after making a sharp cut past her defender. If your eyes are fixed on the ball, you won't be aware of the passing opportunity. Many passing options are there for only an instant before the defense recovers, and that means you have to be able to see the court at all times.

Like most bad habits, dribbling with your head down is most easily stopped before it becomes too engrained. Whenever you practice dribbling, concentrate on keeping your head up as much as possible. The more you do it, the more comfortable you'll become with it, and the less you'll need to have your eyes glued to the ball in order to control it. But be patient—this is a difficult aspect of the game to master. Strive for improvement with each practice. Keep reminding yourself to keep your head up. Work on developing a better feel for the ball. The first time you thread a perfect backdoor pass to a cutting teammate, your satisfaction will make all the practice worthwhile.

Going Both Ways

Talk to any good defensive player and she'll tell you the hardest opponent to guard is one who can beat you a lot of ways—driving, shooting, dribbling, passing; in short, a player who forces the defense to be wary of many different things.

To be an effective dribbler, you must be able to beat your opponent either way—with the right hand or the left. There are countless situations where you'll need your weak hand to drive to the basket or to get out of a tight spot. If you can't go that way without kicking the ball into the third row, you're really only half a player.

Suppose an offensive player has the ball near the left corner. The defender clearly is giving her the baseline; that is, leaving enough room to dribble toward the basket via the baseline. If the offensive player can't control the dribble with her left hand, she's not going to be able to execute this maneuver, and a great chance to score will have been missed. (And if she tries to do it with her right hand, the ball probably will be stolen since she would be leaving the ball unprotected by dribbling to the left with her right hand.)

Being a one-way dribbler hurts you in another way as well. A smart defender will detect that you're "all right" or "all left," and overplay you in that direction, forcing you either to go with your weak hand or not to go at all.

Dribbling with your off hand will feel awkward at first. You'll lose control frequently; it happens to everyone, so don't get too frustrated. When you work at your dribbling, be sure to give at least equal time to your weaker hand. I've seen players who are so uncomfortable dribbling with their off hand that every chance they get—when the coach gets a phone call or looks the other way—they cheat and use their strong hand. It's a cliche, but it's true: They're only cheating themselves.

Don't cheat *yourself*. Keep practicing with your weak hand until you're comfortable with it.

Moves Off the Dribble

Once you're controlling the ball fairly well, it's time to begin working on several moves with the ball that will enable you to shake the toughest defender, giving you room to drive or pass or get free for a shot. Each of these moves must be mastered with both hands. Let's take a look.

Change of Pace

In baseball you'll often see a clever pitcher completely fool a batter by changing the speed of his pitches. Expecting one pitch and getting another, the batter is caught off guard and swings early or late, missing badly. In a similar way, you can fool a defender by changing the speed of your dribble.

Say you're dribbling hard to the basket with your right hand. The defender is staying with you well. How can you shake her? Try a change-of-pace dribble. Slow down abruptly and pull your head and shoulders back ever so slightly, as though you've decided to give up on the drive. As the defender begins to relax—and she almost certainly will once you've stopped

Fig. 7–5 The change-of-pace dribble is a good way to catch a defender off guard. As you approach her *(top)*, slow down and pull back your head and shoulders a little—just enough to make her think you are pulling up. As she relaxes and stands up *(center)*, explode past her with a big step *(bottom)*.

your hard drive—push off hard on your left foot, push the ball out and take off again at high speed. She won't have time to adjust, and you'll explode right past her. This is a very basic move—all you're doing is going from high gear to low gear and back to high gear—but it works remarkably well.

Just make sure your change of pace is abrupt and distinct. Going only moderately fast to moderately slow isn't going to fool anyone. When you begin your move, the defender must think you're dribbling all out. Then when you slow up, she'll momentarily relax and you'll leave her behind when you explode into full speed.

Crossover

The crossover dribble is the fastest way to change directions when you're dribbling, and the best and fastest way to lose your opponent. As you approach the defender (or when the defender forces you to change direction), shift your dribbling hand (in this case, let's say it's your right) from the top to the outside of the ball—just a matter of a few inches toward the right. Pushing hard off your right foot, quickly bounce the ball diagonally in front of you, passing it over to your left hand. Make sure the crossover dribble is low, since it's unprotected as you're switching hands. Quickly shift your weight to the left and change your direction, keeping your shoulder low for extra protection, and cross your right foot over just in front of the defender as you control the ball with your left hand.

A few things to keep in mind: The change in direction must be made sharply. Make the crossover with one hard, low dribble, and shift your weight quickly. Keep your knees flexed as you cut, and accelerate quickly after the crossover has been executed. Basketball is a game of cuts and angles as we've discussed, and the sharper and more precise you make yours, the more success you will have eluding your defender.

Mastering the crossover will allow you to get out of just about any tight spot and get by almost any defender. Not long ago I watched a high school point guard leave behind a trail of defenders all game long. She had only one move—the crossover dribble—but she had it down so well it was all she needed.

Fig. 7–6 A crossover dribble is a good way to change direction and shake a defender. To crossover from your right hand *(left)* to your left, plant your right foot, make a low, hard dribble right in front of your body to your left hand *(center)*, and explode past her *(right)*.

Reverse, or Spin, Dribble

This move should be used when the crossover cannot be, because a defender is too close to risk crossing the ball over in front of her. As you drib-

Fig. 7–7 Use the spin dribble when the defender is too close for you to make the crossover in front of her. To spin toward the left, plant your left leg in front of the defender *(top left),* and dribbling with the right hand, pull the ball back toward your right hip. Quickly bring your right leg around as shown *(top right)* and explode past the defender with the left-hand dribble *(bottom).*

ble (right-handed) facing the defender, plant your left leg and reverse pivot, bringing your right leg around behind you, following the lead of your right shoulder. Still dribbling with the right hand, pull the ball back toward your right hip, being careful not to carry it. Quickly shift it to your left and explode past the defender with the left-hand dribble. Be sure to come hard at the defender before beginning the spin, and make the pivot as sharp as possible. This allows you to "cut off her legs" and get past her before she can react.

Work on technique first when practicing the spin dribble, and worry about speed later. Once you've got it down you'll be able to execute the spin with one dribble, but at the start it's okay to take two or three dribbles. Don't forget to work on spinning using either hand; you want to have as many options as possible to beat your defender.

Dribbling Drills

Crossover

Dribble downcourt and make four distinct crossovers, making sure to change directions sharply with a hard and low crossover dribble. Do the same on the way back, then repeat.

Hesitation and Spin Drill

Make three change-of-pace dribbles as you move the length of the court. Pay attention to form and concentrate on making the changes clear-cut. On your way back, perform three spin dribbles, following the form we discussed. Repeat the drill using your opposite hand for the change of pace as well as the spin.

Full-Court Speed Dribble

Dribble the length of the court as fast as you can, pushing the ball far in front of you and allowing it to come up about waist-high. Dribble with your right hand when going down the court and with the left hand when on the left side. Repeat four times, and go in for a power lay-up after your final run.

Circle Drill

Each player (you can play with any number you like, but the more who play, the bigger the area must be) has a ball in a circle or other defined area. The object is to keep control of your own dribble (protecting the ball with your off arm and by dribbling to the side of your body with the knees flexed) while trying to flick away the ball of the other players. If you deflect another player's ball she is eliminated. Continue the drill until one player remains, then begin again.

A Parting Thought on the Dribble

Players tend to dribble too much at almost every level of basketball. As we've noted, this slows down the offensive flow and often results in other players standing around waiting for the dribbling exhibition to be concluded.

Use the dribble selectively. Resist the temptation to bounce the ball the moment you get it. Remember this golden rule of basketball: Look before you dribble.

Check all your options. Do you have a teammate closer to the hoop to whom you can pass? What cuts are being made? What might open up in a moment or two? Are you in good shooting position? Is there room to drive? Are you being guarded by a player you can beat with the dribble? Is she overplaying you in any direction?

Work on your court awareness so you develop a sense of when and where to use the dribble most effectively. And when you do use it, make sure your eyes are on the court, not the ball. That way you'll be able to react quickly when a scoring or passing opportunity knocks, or when there's a momentary defensive lapse. All good dribblers are heads-up players—literally and figuratively.

Chapter Eight

Making Yourself a Threat— Individual Offense

Your goal as an offensive player is to be as much of a threat as possible to the defense. Everything you do offensively, with and without the ball, should be geared toward this end. You want either to be in a position to score yourself or to make a pass or set a screen that will allow a teammate to score. In this chapter we'll look at some basic ways to make you more difficult to defend against, and thus a more effective offensive player.

Being in Position to Score

The first guideline in making yourself an offensive threat is always to try to receive the ball in scoring position. What that is depends on the player; if you're a center, scoring position is usually close to the basket; if you're a guard, it could well be 18 feet out. The idea is to set up or get open in a place that's within your shooting range, a spot from which you are a threat to score.

This isn't always possible, of course. A teammate might get trapped or be in trouble and you'll have to move 30 feet out to catch a pass from her. In such a situation helping her out naturally takes precedence over getting the ball in scoring position. Nevertheless, you should always be aware of where you are on the court and how you might receive the ball in a scoring position.

Getting Open

No good defensive team is going to let you simply station yourself in a position where you are a real threat to score. Their goal is to keep you and your teammates in a non-threatening position. That means you're going to need to work to get open in the areas on the floor where you want the ball. Let's look at a couple of the best ways to go about it.

The V-Cut

Suppose the ball is at the point. You're on the left wing and your defender is denying you the ball. One good way to get open is to execute a V-cut. Fake a step out toward the perimeter, holding out your right hand as a passing target. As the defender edges out to continue denying you the ball, make a quick change of direction, pushing hard off your right foot, and cut in toward the basket. Hold your left hand out as you cut to give a target to the passer. Make sure you're ready to receive the ball.

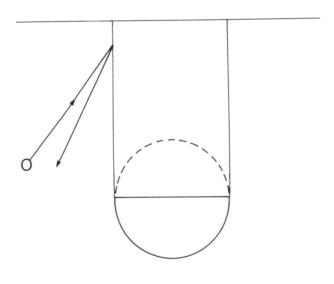

Fig. 8–1 The V-cut is a good way of faking an opponent and getting open for a pass.

Fig. 8–2 The V-cut is an effective way to get yourself free to receive a pass. In the first photo *(top left)* the defender is denying her opponent the ball. To get free, the offensive player executes a V-cut, cutting in sharply toward the basket *(top right)*, then pivoting and popping back out *(bottom)*. Note how her cut has given her room to catch a pass, and how she has her hand out to give the passer a target.

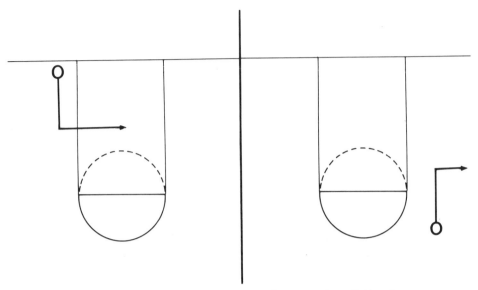

Fig. 8–3   Make sure you make good, hard turns when squaring off. Use these moves to get free of a defender anywhere on the court.

If you're open, the point guard will pass you the ball, and you will have made a successful backdoor cut, meaning you've cut in back of a defender to get free. But let's say she is a very good defender and has managed to stay with you. You're still not open for the pass, so you plant your left, or baseline, foot, push off hard and pop back out on the wing at a good angle to receive the ball in a scoring position. Keep your hands up so you're ready to catch the pass.

That's a V-cut, so called because your two cuts—one in, one back out—resemble the shape of the letter V. V-cuts may be used anywhere on the court. They're very effective for getting free when executed properly with good, abrupt changes of direction.

V-cuts are especially important for players on the wings, who often are denied the ball by the defense. And it's essential for the wings to get open, since most offensive patterns will be started with a pass to them.

Squaring Off

Another useful way to shake free of a defender is to square off. This involves running in a straight line, then stopping, pushing off and making a 90-degree turn. Look at Fig. 8–3. As you can see, square-off cuts, sometimes called L cuts, can be made starting outside and cutting in or starting inside and cutting out. You can turn left or right, depending on where you are and where the ball is.

As with the V-cut, this move depends entirely on how well you execute the change of direction. A lazy, curving turn isn't going to fake anybody out. Concentrate on making your cut hard and sharp, and explode out of the turn to create extra distance from the defense. Give a target and be ready to receive the ball as you cut.

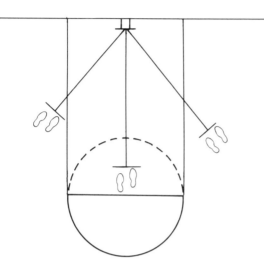

Fig. 8–4 Before shooting, square your shoulders and feet so you're directly facing the basket. If your body isn't squared up, you shouldn't shoot.

Squaring Up

As soon as you receive the ball, pivot so you're directly facing the basket, a move known as squaring up. Why is it so important to square up? Because once you're square to the basket, you're in good triple-threat position—ready to shoot, pass, or dribble. You're not a scoring threat if you're standing sideways to the basket. Nor are you in very good passing position, because you can't see all your passing options. So in effect, failing to square up takes away two of your options—and makes the defender's job much easier.

As you square up, move into triple-threat position: knees flexed, weight evenly distributed on the balls of your feet, shooting foot slightly forward, and the ball well protected, tucked in near the hip of your shooting hand. Positioned in this way, you're able to exercise any of your three options, and the defense must respect all three.

Look Before You Move

It's important to size up the offensive situation before deciding which option to employ. After assuming triple-threat position, check where the defense is, and make sure you know exactly where you are on the court. Both factors have a big bearing on what you may want to do. For example, say you've squared up and you see that the defense has gotten fouled up and there's a wide-open lane to the basket. By all means, take it. Whenever you see room to go toward the basket, go for it. The closer you get to the hoop, the better your chances for making the shot.

Or perhaps there is no glaring opening, but you notice you're just a few feet from the baseline and the defender is leaving you just enough room to drive that way. Again, take it. Anytime the baseline is open to you, don't pass it up. It gives you a big advantage for several reasons: one, your defender is effectively out of the play once you've beaten her that way, because it's difficult for her to recover before you get to the basket; two, unless the other defenders react very quickly, you'll have a lane to drive all the way to the basket; and three, because you've penetrated the defense, even if someone does rush over to stop you, you're probably going to have one or two teammates open underneath. The point to remember is that you have to be alert to exploit advantages such as these.

Now let's look at some moves you can make with the ball that'll help you shake the toughest defender.

One-on-One Offensive Moves

These moves are ways to gain the upper hand on your defender. Once you've gotten the ball and moved into triple-threat position, your aim is to find or create an advantage, then exploit it. If you're going up against a poor defender, you might not need any move at all. Maybe she's laying way off you, and you'll have all the room you need for an uncontested jump shot. Or maybe she's not in a good defensive stance and you can put the ball on the floor and drive right past her to the basket. Whenever you see such opportunities, by all means take them. But when there is not obvious advantage, you're going to need ways to fake your defender into poor position, freeing you to shoot, pass, or dribble. That's what these moves are designed to do.

The Jab Step

Let's say you're right-handed. Establish your left foot as your pivot foot, with your shooting foot slightly in front. (For left-handers, the right foot is the pivot foot and the left foot leads.) This staggered stance is important because it puts you in a ready position to shoot. To execute a jab step, do exactly as the name suggests: take a short, quick jab directly at the defender with your right foot, almost as if you were trying to kick a dime up off the floor. It's important that the jab be short; just move your foot slightly forward. That way, if the defender backs off you, you can go right up for the jumper without bringing your foot back, which gives the defense time to recover. Keep the knees flexed and make the jab convincing—you want the defender to think you're driving hard to the basket.

What happens? How does the defender react? You've got to use your court sense, because what she does will determine what you do next. Let's say (and this will usually be the case) she drops back a few steps when you make your jab because she thinks you're driving to the basket. That's good for you. Her retreating leaves you room to go up for a jump shot. But what if she doesn't react and holds her ground?

Fig. 8–5 The jab step. With a short, quick jab step with her right foot *(center)*, the offensive player gives herself room for a shot. Notice how the defender responds to the fake.

The Rocker Fake

If she doesn't budge, that should tell you one thing: you can beat her with a drive. After all, you've already faked a drive with your jab step, and she didn't react. So now you're going to take advantage and make the drive for real. After the jab step, give a quick fake with your head and shoulders, pulling them upwards and back slightly to make the defender think you're going up for a shot; or that you've decided to stop the drive. This will cause her to tighten up on you or to go up to defend against your shot. After she reacts, take a big, quick first step with your right leg (again, assuming you're a right-handed player). Go right toward her legs and drive hard past her. It's important to "cut off her legs" in this fashion, because if you make your drive wide of her she may have time to recover.

This simple fake works very effectively to freeze the defender so you can drive. The key is giving a good head-and-shoulders fake the moment you

Fig. 8–6 If the defender doesn't back off when you jab step, try the rocker fake. After making the jab *(top right),* give a quick rock backward with your head and shoulders, then explode past her with a big first step *(bottom).*

see she hasn't gone for the jab step, and then exploding past her with that big, quick step. Just be sure to allow the defense time to react to the fake before driving. If you begin driving the instant you finish the head-and-shoulders fake, the defender will not even have had time to be fooled. Pause a moment and let the fake do its work—then explode.

The Crossover

Sometimes you go against a defender who is overplaying you to the strong side—the side you have the ball on. When this occurs, the drive off the rocker fake won't be available, since the defender is lined up in your path. An effective move against an overplaying defender is the crossover (not to be confused with the crossover dribble, though they accomplish the same thing—a quick change of direction).

Using our same example, let's say you have the ball in triple-threat position, and your left foot is the pivot foot. You see she's overplaying you to the right, so it'll be very hard to beat her that way. You try a jab step and she doesn't react. It's time for the crossover. Quickly pick up your right leg and take a big step directly next to her inside (in this case, right) foot and cross the ball over from your right side to your left to protect it and keep it away from the defense. With a strong step, explode past her with a left-hand dribble, keeping your shoulders down to help edge past her. As with the rocker fake, cut close to her so she won't have a chance to catch up to you. Once you've cut off her legs and planted the first key step at her feet, you know you've got her. She either has to foul you or let you go. Just make sure you begin your dribble before you pick up your pivot foot to avoid a traveling violation.

Practice these moves until you can execute them quickly and sharply. Work on them against teammates in practice so you can develop a feel for the different defensive reactions to expect. Remember to make the fakes good and convincing, and to pause just long enough for the defender to be out of position before trying to beat her. When you're driving, cut right at the defender so you can explode past her in a direct path to the hoop.

A Final Word

The moves we've looked at in this chapter are designed to make you more of an offensive threat by two basic means: one, receiving the ball in scoring position; and two, beating the defender so you can get a high-percentage shot. The V-cut and the square-off are simple cuts enabling you to get free to receive the ball within your shooting range. And the one-on-one moves pick up from there, giving you ways to fake the defender out of position so you can shoot or drive to the basket, or at the very least have more room to pass.

Fig. 8–7 This sequence shows the crossover fake, which is valuable when the defense is overplaying you on one side. The offensive player makes her jab step *(top)*, then quickly crosses over in front of the defender with a big step with her right foot, planting it right next to the defender *(center)*. Staying low, she bursts past the defender with a left-hand dribble *(bottom)*.

Don't allow the defense to rest. Make them play you. Always try to get the ball in scoring position, and once you've got it, remember to square up to the basket so you're ready to shoot, pass, or dribble. Look for any and every opportunity when you get the ball. Is there room to shoot? To drive?

Is the defender out of position? If no opportunities are readily available, go to your offensive moves. Try the jab step and go from there, depending on how she plays it. If she retreats, go up for a jumper. If she holds her ground, give a good rocker fake and explode past her. If she's overplaying you, execute the crossover.

The more ways you have to beat your defender, the better will be your chances of scoring. Learning the moves we've looked at in this chapter will give you more opportunities to put the ball in the basket.

Chapter Nine

Working Together— Team Offense

Individual skills are a vital part of the game. Dribbling, shooting, passing—all of them must be mastered if you want to be a complete player.

But that doesn't mean that these skills alone will make you a good basketball player. They won't, because basketball is the ultimate team game. One of the greatest things about the game is that the team with the best players will not always win; the players who mold their talents into the best *team* will. The 1983 Men's NCAA championship game is an excellent case in point. North Carolina State defeated Houston, a team with an awesome collection of talent. Few people gave "the Wolfpack" a chance (I did, since I was rooting with my heart for my alma mater), but they won because they played great team basketball. The moral is that to be a good player, you have to be able to play the game as a part of a team. Let's find out how.

Playing the Percentages

Your goal as a team is to score on every possession, and that means getting the best shot you can every time you move down the court. You don't want to take a 15-footer if a teammate can take a 10-footer, and you don't want to shoot from 10 if someone's free for a lay-up. What can you do as a team player to help your team get the highest-percentage shot?

Hitting the Open Player

If a teammate is open and in better shooting position, always pass her the ball. This is the most basic rule of team basketball, which isn't to say it's easy to do. You're bound to be keyed up when you have the ball in a game. You may be under heavy defensive pressure. You may find it difficult to survey the court for passing opportunities. But you've got to try. Slow yourself down a beat if you feel yourself racing. Take a good look around. The more you do it, the easier it gets.

Don't panic when you get the ball; acting hastily usually yields bad results. With a little composure, you'll be able to see where things might open up. Is the shot there? Is a teammate moving toward an open spot? Can you safely pass her the ball? Is there a defensive weak link you can exploit? Is there a mismatch inside (a tall player on your team being guarded by a much shorter opponent)? Can you beat your defender with the dribble? These are the kinds of things you must try to be aware of. You'll find that your court sense will grow rapidly as you gain more experience.

Maintaining Court Balance

A common mistake among young players is getting bunched up so that two or more teammates are close together on the floor. This interrupts the offensive flow and enables one defender to guard several of your players.

Keep the offense spread out at all times. Force the opponents to defend the entire offensive area. If you see that one area is crowded, cut to another spot. You'll attract defensive attention, and the result could be a scoring opportunity for a teammate, or at the very least, better offensive movement.

Keeping the Ball Moving

When the ball sits, the defense rests. And that's the last thing you want the defense to do. When you get the ball, do something with it. Drive hard for the hoop. Make crisp passes. Force the defense to work to keep up. Not every pass or move will lead directly to a basket, but keeping the ball moving will gradually wear the defense down and increase your chances of getting a better shot. Sometimes four or five simple chest passes from player to player are all it takes to create that good shot you're looking for.

Knowing Your Capabilities

It's important, for your performance as well as the team's, to know your strengths and weaknesses. If you're not a good dribbler, it's unwise to challenge the defense that way. Know which shots are "your" shots and which aren't. You can hurt your team just as much by not taking a shot you should as by taking one you shouldn't. If you have doubts about where and when to shoot, ask your coach. She'll tell you—and be glad you asked. It's a smart question.

Moving Without the Ball

Just as the ball is easier to guard when it's stationary, so are you. It's amazing how some otherwise good players will play as though they're no longer part of the offense after they've gotten rid of the ball. Basketball's a great game to watch, but not when you're on the court. Stay in the flow of things. Do something to keep the defense occupied. Cut to the basket. Clear out an area so a teammate has more room to move. Set a screen to free a teammate. Crash the offensive boards. If a teammate is double-teamed or in trouble, go to the ball and give her a passing outlet so she can safely pass to you.

You're only one of five players, meaning that roughly 80 percent of the time you will be playing without the ball. It's up to you to help the team by using that time constructively. Keep your head up, keep the ball in sight, and above all, keep moving.

Two-Person Plays to Master

Though basketball is a five-person game, some of the most effective offensive plays are worked with just two people. They're easy to learn and highly effective. Good team players recognize situations where the plays can be used and execute the plays crisply.

Give and Go

This is one of the most fundamental plays in basketball. The play can be worked anywhere on the court, with any two players. It couldn't be simpler: you pass (or give) the ball to a teammate, make a fake away from the

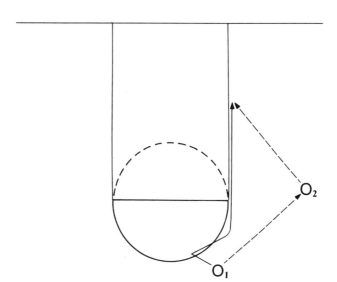

Fig. 9–1 The give-and-go: After passing to teammate O_2, O_1 fakes away, then cuts hard for the hoop and gets the return pass. Make sure you're ready to receive the pass as you cut.

basket (as if you're no longer involved in the play), then quickly "go" to the basket with a sharp cut—ready to receive a return pass. What happens— and the reason it works so well—is that defenders tend to relax when their player gives up the ball. And that inattentive moment is all you need to explode past them.

Timing and making a convincing fake are critical here. It's your job as the cutter to set up the defense so you can get free for the return pass. If you fake and cut immediately upon passing the ball, the move may look automatic and not fool the defender. Give her a moment to relax once you've given up the ball. Pause a beat or two, make a sharp fake away, then change directions and go to the basket with an explosive burst.

Make sure you look for the ball as you cut, and give the passer a target by keeping your hands up. You'll probably be open for only a second, and you must be ready to catch the ball.

Back Door

This is the move to use if the defense is really overplaying the perimeter passing lanes. Look at the photos in Fig. 9–2. Notice how the defender is

Fig. 9–2 If a defender is denying you the ball, try going backdoor on her—that is, cutting behind her back toward the basket. Note how the defender is overplaying the passing lane *(top left)*. The offensive player takes a couple of quick steps away from the basket to draw her opponent out *(top right)*, then pivots *(bottom left)* and cuts hard for the hoop, giving the passer a target as she goes *(bottom right)*. Her backdoor cut—marked by a quick pivot and a good, sharp change of direction—has freed her to receive a pass close to the basket.

trying to cut off the pass by edging into the passing lane between passer and receiver. But see what she's done by doing this? She has left herself vulnerable to a backdoor cut (a cut made behind the defender toward the hoop).

To make a good backdoor move, take a step toward the outside passing lane as shown (this will draw the defender out with you), then change direction and cut right behind her for the hoop. Keep your head and hands up as you cut, so you're set to catch the pass. The back door is a great move to try anytime the defense is pressuring you to deny you the ball. If she's that close to you, it means it's going to be easy to cut behind her into the open. Few defensive players will be able to keep up with you, particularly if you disguise your intentions by setting them up with that step to the outside.

Setting Screens

A well-set screen makes things tough on the defense. It's hard enough stopping a player from scoring without having to fight through a block, which is all a screen is.

To set a screen (or "pick"), plant your body perpendicular to the defender (so her shoulder is lined up with the center of your body) and at least a foot away from her. Your feet should be wider than your shoulders to take up as much space as possible, and the knees should be flexed to absorb the impact and maintain good balance after contact. Keep your arms in, both for protection (when you're bumped by the defender) and to prevent blocking the defender with your arms, which is a foul.

Fig. 9–3 For best results when setting a screen, position yourself perpendicular to the defender, keeping the knees bent and the legs slightly more than shoulder-width apart.

The idea in screening is to free a teammate for a shot, drive, or pass. For it to work, the teammate must do two things: one, she must occupy the defender and set her up for the screen by taking her away (as if she's going in a different direction); and two, she must make a good, sharp cut off the pick to get her defender off stride ("rub her off"). If the teammate runs wide of the pick, the defender will slip through without losing a step.

You can screen anywhere on the court and anytime a teammate needs more playing room. You can do it by moving toward the ball or away from the ball. Screening on the ball is simply moving toward your teammate who has the ball and setting the screen so she can "cut" off you. Screening away is when you move away from the ball and set your screen for another player so that she will then be free to get a pass. That's the most effective place to screen, because many defenders relax when they're playing off the ball, making them easy to rub off so your teammate can cut into the open. Screening away also helps maintain good court balance by keeping players spread out, as well as improving the offensive flow, since more players are moving and involved in the play.

Fig. 9–4 Screening away from the ball. Note the wide stance that makes it harder for the defender to get through, and how her knees are bent for better balance *(left)*. After setting the screen, she rolls the basket, giving a passing target and looking for the ball (right).

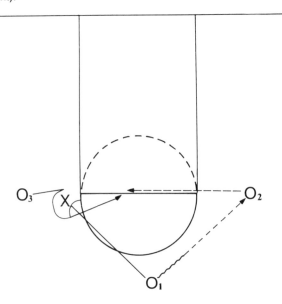

Fig. 9–5 This diagram shows screening away from the ball. O_1 passes to O_2, then moves away to set a screen for O_3. After faking her defender, O_3 comes off the screen and receives a pass from O_2.

Looking for the Roll

Whenever you screen, always be alert for an opportunity to "roll" to the basket. Say a teammate is at the elbow of the key (the corner of the free-throw line and the side of the key), trying to get open for a pass. You move up and set a screen for her. She takes her defender away, setting her up for the screen, then cuts sharply off you. As she comes by, her defender gets bumped into you. That's when you should pivot toward the ball and roll toward the basket, almost as if the cutter had tossed a rope around you and was pulling you along with her. Often you'll be more open than the cutter because of the way the defensive assignments get messed up by the screen.

When rolling, be sure to have your hands up to give the passer a target, and try to use your body to keep your defender behind you. As long as you maintain this position, you're in good position to receive a pass.

Remember in setting a pick that the defender's shoulders should be aligned with the middle of your stance; this maximizes your ability to screen her. You won't be able to rub her off if you're right alongside her. Also remember, when you're the one cutting, to cut off the pick as sharply as possible. Cutting wide is wasted motion that makes the play easier to defend against. It's the cutter's job to occupy the defender, taking her away from the screen so it will work more effectively. Thus, if a teammate is picking for you to your left, fake a move to the right to take your defender away, then change direction, explode to the left, and run her into the block.

If you're ever in doubt about what to do when you don't have the ball, set a screen for a teammate. You can't go wrong with it. It's difficult to defend against, and leads to two good passing options: to the cutter or to you, as you roll toward the basket.

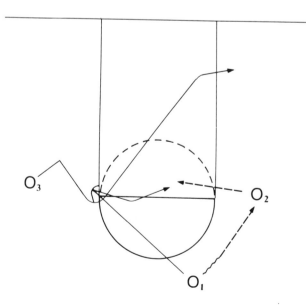

Fig. 9–6 Rolling off a screen: O_1 passes to O_2, then screens away for O_3, who cuts hard to the basket. Just after O_3 uses the screen, O_1 rolls open toward the ball, giving a target and looking for a pass from O_2.

The Fast Break

Few aspects of basketball are as dependent on good teamwork as the fast break. To make the break work, a team needs good rebounding, passing, timing, and quickness. It's a demanding style of play, but its rewards are tremendous. A fast-breaking style can put points on the board and demoralize your opponents faster than anything. I've watched games where three or four quick baskets off the break have changed the entire flow of the action.

How the Break Works

The idea behind the fast break is simple: beat your opponent downcourt. If you do that, you can run a play before they set up their defense. Ideally, on a break you have a 3-on-2 or 2-on-1 player advantage, and that means you should get a very-high-percentage shot at the basket.

First Things First

You can't run without the ball. If you don't have a good rebounding team, forget about fast breaking. The whole style of play is predicated on having one or two players who dominate the boards and allow other players to make the quick break. (You also can start a break after a steal or any change of possession, but since rebounding is the most common way of gaining possession, that's the one indispensable ingredient to being able to run the break consistently.)

Once your team has the rebound, the next key is the outlet pass—the pass the rebounder makes to a player (almost always a guard) who is waiting in the flat (the area from the free-throw line, extended, to the baseline). Throwing a good outlet pass is critical to the break. It must be made quickly so you can get the jump on the opponent right away. To make a quick release of the outlet pass, the rebounder should pivot away from the basket and throw an overhead pass, snapping the ball as sharply as she can to her teammate, who is moving to an open spot and giving a target away from the defense. Bringing the ball down and throwing a chest pass wastes precious seconds.

Hitting High Gear

Okay, the break is initiated by the outlet pass. Here are some important things to keep in mind to run it properly:

•Look upcourt. That's where you're going (as quickly as possible). If a teammate is open ahead of you, pass her the ball.

•Always be ready to pass first, dribble second. We've seen that passing is the fastest way to advance the ball, and speed is of the essence on the break. The slightest hesitation may be all the defense needs to catch up to you and take away your advantage.

•Get the ball to the center of the court. The defense has to work harder when you move the ball to the middle. This gives you more attacking room, since you can pass either left or right, and makes the defense cover more of the court.

•Fill the lanes. The player in the middle needs someone to pass to, so spread out and fill the left and right lanes flanking the middle. Get out on the break quickly, sprinting from foul line to foul line to make sure the player with the ball has a good passing angle to you.

•Stay wide, then cut for the basket. When you're running an outside lane, be sure to stay well away from the middle. If you edge in too close, one defender can guard both you and your teammate in the middle. Maintain this wide position until you reach the top of the key, then cut diagonally for the basket. Do this by planting the outside foot and pushing off, changing directions and going toward the hoop at a 45-degree angle. This makes you a prime passing target for a power lay-up or an easy 45'er—a short jumper off the board.

•Communicate! When players are moving at high speed, it's more important than ever that they know where their teammates are. If you're trailing behind the play, yell, "Trailer." If you're open on the right, yell, "Right." Let your teammates know about every advantage you see.

•Force the defense to react. As she gets to the foul line, the player with the ball in the middle must make the defense commit itself. If nobody picks her up, she should drive all the way to the basket. If someone does guard her, she should pull up quickly with a jump stop and look to hit one of the cutters with a bounce pass.

•Deciding whether to drive or pass is a split-second judgment the middle player has to make. If she's free, she goes to the hoop. If she's pressured, she stops, because it means one of the wings must be open. After making the pass, the middle player should cut to the elbow of the lane she has just passed to. This puts her in position for a pass if the wing is unable to get off a shot. If she gets the ball back, she has the option of taking a jumper, reversing the court and passing to the wing on the other side, or pulling the ball back out and setting up the regular offense.

•Have a trailer. Hustle downcourt even if you're not in the first wave of fast-breakers. Often the defense will stop the initial break, but by following the play as a trailer, you can receive a pass, grab an offensive rebound and help your team reassert its advantage. The trailer often is open at the elbow, or as she cuts down the lane.

When a fast break is run properly and you have a clear advantage over the defense, you should get one of four potential shots off the break: a power lay-up, a 45'er, or a jumper from either the elbow or baseline (after reversing the ball from one wing to the other). If none of these is readily available, it's much better to bring the ball out and set up the regular offense, rather than forcing the issue.

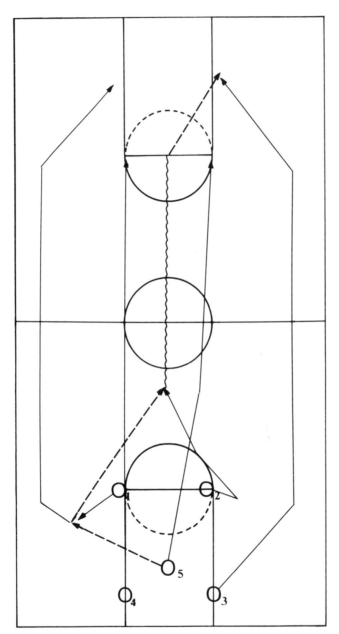

Fig. 9–7 A diagram of a well-run fast break. O_5 gets the rebound and makes an outlet pass to O_1, who passes to O_2 cutting into the middle. O_2 dribbles to the free-throw line while O_1 and O_3 hustle downcourt to fill the outside lanes and O_4 and O_5 act as trailers. O_2 jump stops at the free-throw line and makes a crisp bounce pass to O_3, who is cutting for the basket at a 45-degree angle.

It's primarily the responsibility of the middle player to recognize when to keep breaking and when to slow things up.

The fast break takes a lot of practice to work smoothly. Running it properly requires good passing (an overhead to the outlet, a bounce pass to a cutting wing); sharp cuts by the wings; and a quick reading of the court situation by the middle player. Her teammates must know where the ball is, remember to present a good passing target, and be able to catch the ball on the move.

Because it's a high-speed offense, the fast break is risky and increases the chance of a turnover. Only good ball-handling teams should consider fast-breaking; otherwise the up-tempo style will do you more harm than good. Teams should always play to their strengths. For instance, if your team has a front line of tall, strong inside players, it would be foolish to fast-break. Better to slow the pace down and play a setup offense so you can take full advantage of your inside game.

A Final Word

Team basketball is all about playing to your strengths and taking advantage of your opponent's weaknesses. If your team is fast and you also have a good rebounder or two, use the fast break. If you're tall and strong but slower, take your time and work it inside. Learn to think in team terms about what you can contribute to make the team play better. If your center has a big height advantage over her opponent, keep feeding the ball inside until the opponents show they can stop her. If someone on your team has hit four in a row, try to give her the ball: You might as well go with the hot hand. Always go with the percentages. Look to get the best shot you can. Take whatever the defense gives you. Keep the ball moving. Make the other team work.

Whatever you do, keep active all the time. Concentrate on always doing something constructive for your team—with and without the ball. Look for give-and-go's. Set picks away from the ball. Cut for the basket. Crash the offensive boards. Keep the ball moving. Look for cutting teammates, and keep your head up so you're alert to defensive weaknesses. Is the defense spread out, and thus clear for a pass to the middle? Is it vulnerable on the baseline? Is it conceding the jump shot?

Your goal—putting the ball in the basket—is simple enough. But to accomplish it consistently, you need five players working together. By playing alertly and unselfishly, you make yourself and your teammates more threatening offensive players. A good team is much better than the sum of its parts—and a lot harder to stop than a collection of talented individuals.

Chapter Ten

Playing Tough Defense

There's a great thing about defense: You get back exactly what you put into it. If you work at it, defense will never take a night off.

You'll often hear coaches say, "Defense, not offense, keeps you in games." Why? Because even Carol Blazejowski, one of the finest shooters in women's basketball, had games when the ball just wouldn't fall. And when your shots aren't falling, it's either play tough defense or get blown out. Nobody ever said you had to score a lot to win—you just need more points than the opposition. That's why the best offense is a good defense.

Alertness is a key ingredient to good defense. The slightest lapse in concentration can lead to two points for the opposition. The offensive player knows what she's going to do and where she's going to go. Will she drive? Pull up for a shot? Make a cut? Pass to a teammate? You don't know, so stopping her depends on anticipating what she might do. It also depends on quick reactions, good footwork, proper positioning, and plain old hard work.

Playing Aggressive Defense

Too often defense is taught as a purely "reactive" part of the game. That is, you react to what the offense does in order to stop them. Good defense involves quick reactions, sure; but it also involves quick and aggressive *actions*—moves that force the offense to react, instead of the other way around. By turning the tables in this way, you can cause turnovers, disrupt the offensive flow and force the offense to take low-percentage shots.

Don't play a passive defense of purely reaction. Take the initiative. Be aggressive. Denying the ball to your opponent, making her change her course, sealing off the baseline, overplaying her so she must use her weak hand to dribble—these are just some of the aggressive actions you can take on defense that will force the offense to react. Aggressive defense will shake their confidence, make them play tentatively and shift their focus from what they want to do to what you might do.

There are two basic types of defensive situations: on the ball and off the ball. On the ball is when the player you're guarding has the ball, and off the ball is when one of the four other offensive players has it. Let's look at the right technique for each.

On-the-Ball Defense

You must be ready to move quickly in any direction when your opponent has the ball. Your knees are flexed, your back is straight and your weight

Fig. 10–1 The basic stance for on-the-ball defense. Note how the defender's knees are flexed so she can move and react quickly. Her back is straight, and her hands are out to occupy the passing lanes.

is on the balls of your feet (stay off your heels; they are to defense what the palm is to shooting—big trouble). Your rear end should be low, as shown in the accompanying photo; the bend is at the knees, not the waist. You can't move nearly as quickly when you're bending at the waist because it leaves you poorly balanced, with your head over your toes. Proper defensive stance is almost a seated position, so that if I tucked a chair under you you would settle easily into it.

This position allows you to move with maximum quickness, which is critical to playing good D. Basketball involves actions and reactions; the quicker you are, the better defender you'll be.

Foot position is also extremely important. Your feet should be about shoulder-width apart and staggered, one foot slightly ahead of the other. Which foot is in front depends on which way the opponent is moving. When she's dribbling with her right hand, it's your right foot that's up front; when she's dribbling with the left, it's your left foot that's forward. (Another way to remember the correct foot position is to keep your midline foot—that is, the foot closest to the middle of the court—forward.) In this position, you're able to move your feet quickly, as well as force your opponent to the outside, giving her a longer path to the basket and a less threatening offensive position.

Shuffling

Maintaining good, well-centered defensive position isn't easy. If it were, basketball wouldn't be such a high-scoring game. Cutting off your opponent's path requires covering ground swiftly and efficiently while still being able to change directions instantly. Doing all this calls for a kind of footwork that's the heart of on-the-ball defense—the defensive shuffle. The shuffle consists of quick, choppy sidesteps, with the legs flexed (no bouncing up and down—that's wasted motion) and the head stationary and the feet roughly shoulder-width apart.

Say your opponent is driving to her right. From your defensive stance, you move the left foot out to the left and quickly shuffle your right foot in the same direction. If she stops and cuts the other way, make a drop step (we'll see how in a moment) and keep shuffling with the same short, choppy steps. Be sure to keep them short; long, sliding-type steps significantly slow your reaction time.

Don't cross your feet when you're playing on-the-ball defense. Putting one foot over another is a slower movement that can easily leave you tangled up or off balance. The shuffle step is far more efficient. It keeps you well-balanced and braced to move whichever way your opponent does because with the short steps your feet are almost constantly in contact with the floor.

The only time you should cross your legs is when your player has beaten you and you have to catch up, or when you're sprinting a long distance up

Fig. 10–2 Use the drop step to stay with a dribbler when she changes direction. In the first photo *(top left)*, the defender is guarding her opponent in a staggered stance with the left foot back. When the dribbler changes direction, the defender quickly drops the right foot backward *(top right)* and regains good position *(bottom)*.

or across court. For such straight bursts, use your regular running motion. But as soon as you get close to the player, shift quickly into shuffling.

Executing the Drop Step

Suppose your opponent is dribbling to her right. You're staying with her in proper defensive position, knees flexed and the right foot slightly in front of the left. You shuffle over and beat her to the spot, causing her to change direction and go to her left. In order to maintain good defensive position, you must execute a move known as the drop step.

Pushing off with your left foot, quickly open your hips by dropping your right foot backward. For extra momentum as you open up, swing your elbow (in this case the right one) in the direction of the drop step. Shuffle your left foot over and keep in your good, low defensive coil with the left foot up, since your opponent is now going left. With this simple pivot, you've changed directions as quickly as possible and prevented your opponent from getting by you.

When the change of direction is from left to right, the drop step involves the same movements in reverse. Your left foot is up when you're defending the left-hand dribble, so here you swing back your left elbow, push off the right foot and open up with a backward step of your left foot.

No matter which way you're pivoting with your drop step, make sure the first step after it is an explosive one, since you need all the speed you can get at that point to maintain good defensive position. For maximum explosiveness, push off your front leg, your power source. The momentum from the hard push-off helps get you going after the change.

Defensive Positioning

When your opponent has the ball well outside her scoring range, your hands are held palms up, a foot or so outside the knee. Proper hand position is important; not only does it help maintain good balance, it discourages passes by filling space in the passing lanes and it leaves you ready to flick away the ball if the defender loses control. As a general rule, you should be within an arm's length of your opponent. If you can't touch the opposing player with your arm held out straight, you're too far away. This is only a rule of thumb, however. If your opponent is quicker than you, lay off her another step to make it harder for her to beat you.

Your goal is to stay well-centered in front of your opponent so the ball is aligned roughly in the middle of your stance. Do that and you'll beat her to the spot she wants to reach and make her go the other way.

One point about the arms: the closer you are to the basket, the higher you should hold one arm (not both, because that makes it too hard to move). When guarding someone within her shooting range, you must constantly be ready to defend against a shot, and if your arm is up you're in much better position to do so. This also helps keep the ball out of the key by closing off passing lanes.

Keeping Your Opponent Away from the Basket

The object of good on-the-ball defense is to keep the opponent as far from the basket as possible. You want to force her to take a low-percentage shot (or no shot at all), rather than one close to the hoop. The key to doing this is cutting off her path to the basket. Stay well-centered in front of your opponent, between her and the basket, and force her to take a longer—and less threatening—route to where she wants to go. Not only does this enable you to shut off the drive, it discourages her from making passes inside the key and it puts you in good position to contest a shot if she tries shooting from the outside.

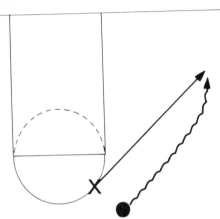

Fig. 10–3 Effective on-the-ball defense forces your opponent to take a longer route to the basket than she wants to. In the diagram, note how X has funneled her opponent away from the basket.

Off-the-Ball Defense

Defense isn't over when your opponent gets rid of the ball. Just because she no longer has it doesn't mean she's not a threat. She could suddenly cut to the hoop and get a pass for an easy lay-up. She could run over and set a screen away from the ball. She could do any number of things to help her team score. To stop her, you have to keep an eye on her as well as an eye on the ball.

Retreat Step

After your opponent passes the ball, the first thing to do is take a big step back *in the direction of the pass*, a move known as a retreat step. This puts you in a position to defend against a cut to the basket, as well as to support your teammate in case she needs help.

See the Ball

You must always know where the ball is when you're playing defense; thus your positioning changes whenever either the ball or your opponent moves. The best way to defend a player without the ball is with positioning we call ball-you-man. You have to keep track of both to play sound defense.

Your exact position depends on where on the court the ball and your opponent are. Look at the accompanying diagrams. You want to set up so there's an imaginary triangle between you, the ball, and your opponent. As a rule, the closer your player is to the ball, the closer you should be to her. Thus, if the ball is only one pass (8 to 10 feet or so) away, you should lay off her no more than a few feet, edging toward the ball just a little and holding the arm closest to the ball out so that your hand, with the palm turned outward, is in the passing lane.

Now let's say the ball is on the other side of the court. To maintain that desired triangle, you must move away from your opponent, opening up your stance so you can use your peripheral vision to see both ball and man. Why do you set up farther away when the ball is cross-court? For a couple of reasons. One, your opponent is not much of a threat to get a pass when the ball is so far away, so you don't have to be as concerned about that. Two, this "sagging off" puts you in a position to help out defensively in another area. Suppose you're guarding one forward and the other forward has the ball in the corner. She beats her defender and begins driving to

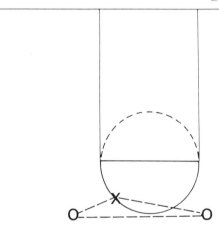

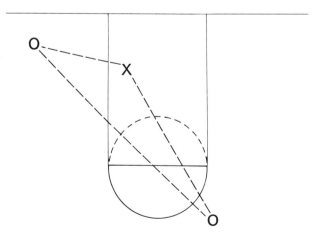

Fig. 10–4 When playing defense off the ball, position yourself to form an imaginary triangle between you, the ball, and your opponent. The farther the ball is from your opponent, the farther you should sag off her and the closer you should be to the ball. This allows you to see both your opponent and the ball and to provide support for your teammates.

the hoop. Since you're sagging off, you're close enough to move over and pick up the driving player and prevent her from going in uncontested. You wouldn't be able to do this if you stayed close to your own opponent. This sort of helping out, or *support*, as we call it, is a hallmark of a sound defensive team. By constantly supporting one another, players accomplish two important defensive objectives: one, they're always in position to pick up an opponent threatening to score; and two, they're able to guard the middle of the court by filling the lane so it's difficult for the offense to penetrate for high-percentage shots. Proper off-the-ball defense enables you to accomplish both.

It's important to remember that defense is a team game. It doesn't do your team much good if you shut out your opponent but some other player fires in 35 and you lose. You have to think in terms of *your* team stopping *their* team, and that means giving support. You must always be aware of the most dangerous offensive threat: the player with the ball. If a player beats her defender and is moving in for an uncontested lay-up, you've got to react quickly and get in position to challenge her.

Make sure when playing off the ball that you always know where both the ball and your opponent are. Remember that the closer you are to the ball, the greater the chance your opponent will get it, and the tighter you must guard her. On the other hand, when the ball is cross-court, maintain the triangle we discussed by opening your stance and dropping off a couple

Fig. 10-5 Deny your opponent possession when she's only one pass away from the ball. Keep your arm nearest the ball slightly flexed and positioned so it's in the passing lane. Make sure you keep your knees bent, and position yourself so you can see both the ball and your opponent.

of steps toward the middle, seeing both your player and the ball. Be ready to give support at all times. Good defense requires total effort by all five players.

Ball Denial and Lane Denial

The best way to defend your opponent is not to let her get the ball, and to stop her from going where she wants to go. These defensive tasks are known as ball denial and lane denial.

To deny your player the ball, set up so your hand is just barely in the passing lane—the imaginary line between the ball and the player you're guarding. Staying in a good, well-balanced defensive stance, hold the arm that's closer to the ball away from your body but with the elbow still flexed (if you extend the arm fully you won't be able to react soon enough when the ball is passed). Keep the palm turned out so you can deflect the ball if it is passed to your opponent. When you deny your player the ball in this way, the passer will probably look for another target, which is just what

Fig. 10–6 As a general rule, the closer your opponent is to the basket, the more important it is to deny her the ball. Here the defender is fronting her opponent, meaning that she has set up so that she is entirely in the passing lane. The only way a pass can get through is if the ball is lobbed over the defender's head.

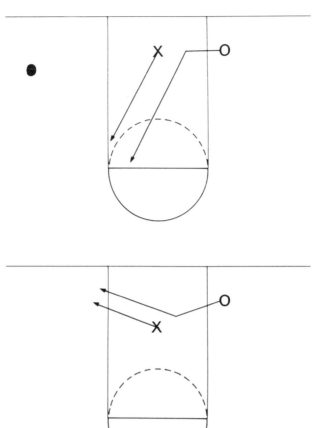

Fig. 10–7 To deny dangerous lane cuts when you're on defense, force your opponent away from the ball, as shown. When the ball is low (top diagram), force the cutter to go high. When the ball is high (bottom diagram), make the cutter go low.

you want. You have made the offense look for other options and taken away part of their game plan.

The closer your opponent is to the basket, the more important ball denial becomes. Why? Because if your opponent gets the ball three feet from the hoop she has a high-percentage shot, as well as several open passing lanes. So, if you're guarding a player who is working close to the basket, you must set up so most of your body (not just your hand) is in the passing lane. And when you're guarding a low post (who usually sets up at the first box at the side of the free-throw lane), you must keep your *entire* body in the passing lane, as shown in Figure 10–6. This is known as fronting your opponent, and as you can see, it makes every pass impossible except for a high-arching lob. If that pass is thrown, you should get help from the weak side—the side of the defense away from the ball. Ball denial works by discouraging the offense from making the pass, and forcing them to look for another option.

In lane denial, you're trying to force your opponent to go where she doesn't want to go. With quick actions and reactions and good, hard defensive shuffling, you can take away the lane she wants by beating her to the spot she's headed for. Where should you force her? Away from the ball (notice how everything in defense hinges on your knowing where the ball is). Never let her have a direct path to the ball. If the ball is high, that is, above the foul line, force her to cut low. If the ball is low, force her to go high.

Once you're cut off her path, she'll probably change direction and try cutting behind you. If she does, execute a drop step, pivoting so you can see the ball as you feel behind you for your cutting opponent. Opening up in this way allows you to continue denying the pass (or if it is thrown, to intercept it), thus forcing your opponent to cut out of the three-second (free-throw) lane to a less dangerous part of the court.

When we looked at offense, we talked about how you want to make sharp cuts and take the shortest routes you can, to both the ball and the basket. On defense, that's exactly what you want to deny. Cut off the shortest route to the ball. Make the pass as hard as possible to complete. It's not easy. It takes great alertness and a lot of hard work, but you'll reap big dividends for your efforts. When they're unable to go where they want and get the ball where they want, many players become frustrated. Soon they're taking poor shots and forcing their passes, and gradually their whole offensive rhythm gets disrupted. That's exactly what you, the defense, want.

Anticipate

Quickness is a tremendous asset on defense, but it's not everything. You can become a first-rate defensive player even if you're not extremely quick. You can do it by being smart and learning to anticipate when and where a pass might be made, your opponent might cut, or in which direction a play is going to be run.

Say you've noticed your opponent has tried driving to the right three straight times early in the game. The next time she gets the ball, you overplay her, moving a half-step to your left to take away her right-hand drive. You've anticipated where she'll go and taken it away from her. She tries the drive and winds up charging into you. She gets a foul. You get the ball.

Or perhaps you're guarding a player one pass away from the ball. During the entire game their point guard has passed the ball to your opponent from the same spot. So you cheat a little. Knowing your opponent is a good bet to get the ball, you edge forward to cover more of the passing lane. As the ball is passed, you uncoil from your stance and pick the ball off by deflecting it with your hand (which you've got in the passing lane, with the palm out—just for this purpose), moving quickly to recover it and dribbling it downcourt for an easy lay-up. The steal is possible because you correctly anticipated where and when the pass would be thrown. It's always fun to gamble on defense; making steals adds to the excitement of playing tough D.

Fig. 10–8 The screen is set, but the defender does a good job of fighting over the top *(top)*. Anticipating her opponent's cut, the defender reacts quickly and moves so that she doesn't get rubbed off by the screen *(center)*. The offensive player is looking for the ball *(bottom)*, but the defender is still in good position to deny it.

Defending Screens

A screen, you'll remember, occurs when a player plants herself next to a defender, setting a block to free a teammate. A good offensive team will set dozens of screens in a game. What do you do?

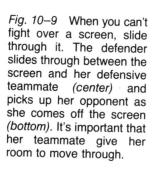

Fig. 10–9 When you can't fight over a screen, slide through it. The defender slides through between the screen and her defensive teammate *(center)* and picks up her opponent as she comes off the screen *(bottom)*. It's important that her teammate give her room to move through.

The first step is to make sure the pick is called out. This is done by the player guarding the opponent who is setting the screen. Usually she'll say, "Pick left" or "Pick right," and this will alert you that the other team is trying to screen you.

Ideally, you will be able to "fight over" the pick. Reacting as soon as the pick is called, shuffle with your player as she moves toward the pick, staying low and well balanced. Fight your way over it, maintaining a position between your opponent and the screen.

If you can't fight over (sometimes it's impossible if the cutter moves very close to the pick), "slide through" the pick by slipping behind it and moving laterally to guard your opponent when she gets to the other side of it. To have room to do this, the defender guarding the screen must step back, allowing space for you to get through. She also should step into the path of the cutter to slow her down—a move known as "exposing." This causes the offensive player to hesitate, giving you a chance to slide through and cover her again before she can get free. If your opponent stops directly behind the screen, she probably will get a fairly open shot at the basket. But better to concede that than to get bumped off by the screen and have your player drive in for a lay-up or short jumper.

If you're unable to fight over or slide through, your last option against the screen is to "switch," a move in which you and your teammate guarding the screen change assignments: She picks up your player after you've been screened off and you pick up the screener.

It's best to stay with your opponent by fighting over or sliding through a screen. Switching should be the last option, since it often leads to defensive mismatches. If you're a 5-foot-4 guard who is screened by a 6-foot center, and your center switches, you end up guarding a player eight inches taller than you, which a smart opponent will take advantage of. Of course, switching is better than letting your player go in for an easy lay-up, but the best defense is to react early, work hard and fight your way over the top or slide through between the screen and your teammate guarding her.

Guarding Against the Roll

When you're the one guarding the screen, you must also be ready to defend the screener when she rolls after the cutter has used her. If she rolls to the basket, react quickly and stay with her, pivoting so you never lose sight of the ball. Move around her quickly so you can get a hand in the passing lane by fighting to stay between your opponent and the ball.

Hints for Better Defense

• Know your opponent. Look for tendencies, habits, and weaknesses in her style of play, and try to make her change her game. If she drives only to the left, make her go right. If she only likes to drive, lay off her a couple of feet and make her shoot from the outside. The more your force her to do things she's not comfortable with, the better the chance she'll get off her game.

• Don't reach in. It's very tempting to stick out your arm and try to take the ball away. It's also bad defense, because the reach-in foul is probably the most frequent infraction whistled by officials. Reaching in is lazy and leaves you overextended and off balance—ready to be exploited by a smart opponent.

•Move your feet and stop your opponent by forcing her away from the basket. Be aggressive and go for the ball if you think you can get it. Keep your hands out and flick the ball upward. But don't just take a wild stab and hope for the best. Even if you don't foul, it'll look as though you did and will put you in poor defensive position besides.

•Shut off the baseline. When we looked at offense, we said you should take the baseline every time the defense gives it to you. On defense you want to deny it to your opponent for the same reasons: A player driving the baseline usually leads to a lay-up and/or a foul. When you're near that part of the court, overplay toward the baseline so your opponent won't have that option. It's not ideal if she beats you driving toward the middle either, but it's a lot less dangerous because there's more defensive help in the middle.

•Watch the midsection. A good offensive player will try to fake you with her foot, head, shoulder, the ball, you name it. But she can't fake you

Fig. 10–10 Defending against a shot. The defender has her hand up, ready to contest a shot. Note how the arm is straight up, not into the shooter.

with her stomach. Wherever it goes, she'll go. Don't fall for all the fakes and pumps; zero in your attention on the middle of the body and you won't be fooled.

- Put your hands up in close. It's okay to play your opponent with your hands relatively low (outside your knees, as we discussed) when you're far from the basket. But when you're within her shooting range, say 15 feet or closer, keep at least one hand at shoulder height. That way, if she attempts a shot you'll be able to distract her. Remember to keep the elbow bent. This allows for quick reaction when a shot does go up, and it also can fool an opponent into thinking she has room to shoot by concealing a few inches of your reach. Fully extended, you may block the shot she thought she could get over you. If your elbow's locked, however, you won't be able to move your arm quickly enough to distract her.
- Know the difference between a smart foul and a dumb one. A smart foul is when the score is close and an opponent is going up for a lay-up and you're the only one who can stop her. If you foul her, so what? She gets two free throws, but chances are she would've had a sure two points anyway if you'd just let her go. A dumb foul is a reach-in, a needless bump, pushing off an opponent with your hand instead of moving your feet, or fouling a shooter who is taking a low-percentage shot.
- Be aggressive, not reckless. A good defensive team really comes after the offense, guarding them tightly, playing the passing lanes, looking for steals. Work hard, concede nothing, play with aggressiveness, but make it controlled aggressiveness. You get only five fouls per game. You can't afford picking up stupid ones by being overly physical. I've seen lots of players who hustle relentlessly but spend a good part of their time on the bench simply because they don't know the difference between playing hard and playing recklessly.
- Don't leave your feet until the ball is in the air. If you're continually jumping up and down, you're not playing good defense. Every moment you're off the ground is a moment for your opponent to get around you. Stay grounded, where you can stick right with her, and don't leap until you're sure she's going up with the ball.
- Use the drop step to change directions so you can stick with your opponent when she makes sharp cuts.
- When the dribble stops, swarm. If your opponent gives up the dribble, you should be all over her. She can't drive around you since she's already used her dribble. Get your hands up in the passing lanes, and make it as difficult as possible for her to see. Use your arms to prevent her from making a pass or taking a shot. Under such pressure most players will panic and make a hasty pass just to get you off their backs.
- Talk. Good defensive teams communicate constantly. They'll say, "Help" if their player gets by them; "Shot" when the ball is headed for the hoop; "Watch baseline" if they think the opponent is going to make a move there; or "Pick left" or "Pick right" when a screen is being set. It keeps

everyone alert and makes for quick adjustments when the opponent is threatening.

•Block, don't swat. When you go up to defend a shot, hold your arm straight overhead as high as you can, and simply try to distract the shooter. That's all it takes to make the shot miss. Don't swat at the ball and swing your arm forward into the shooter. You may get the ball; you will also get a foul.

•Know where you are on the floor. If you're guarding a dribbler high (above the foul line), force her away from the middle so she must take the long way to the basket. If you're near the baseline, seal it off and make her go another way. Always try to deny the offense the most direct route to the basket. If you're playing off the ball close in, be ready to deny the ball by keeping part or all of your body in the passing lane. Force cutters to move away from the ball. Keep a hand up if your opponent has the ball within her shooting range. Know at all times where the ball is and where your opponent is.

A Final Word

Defense isn't glamorous. A top scorer always will draw more raves than a top defensive player. But good defense wins as many games, or more, than good offense does. And as we've seen, you can never tell when your shooting touch may take the night off.

Good defense breeds other good things. It gets you in the flow of the game. It can provide a big lift, generating momentum for your offense. It carries over into other phases of the game. Fueled by your success in shutting down an opponent, you tend to rebound, pass, run the offense—play the whole game with sharper concentration and better execution.

Good D is hard work. It's also fun. Stopping another team from scoring gives you tremendous satisfaction. You get pumped up, and you know your efforts have paid off in a big way. Defense keeps you in every game, and that's a great guarantee to have.

Take pride in your defense. By working hard, you make the other team earn every point. You disrupt their offensive rhythm. You get them flustered by preventing them from doing what they want the way they want. And you gradually wear them down. They get tired physically from having to work so hard for their points, and they get tired mentally of having a hand in their face all game long. Perhaps most important of all, they begin to have doubts about whether they can score on you. They become tentative—and less effective. In the final minutes of a close game, I'll go with the team that plays the tougher defense every time. Defense may not get acknowledged or applauded nearly enough, but it's a fun way to play, and it wins a lot of games.

I'd say that's a good return for your effort.

Chapter Eleven

Under the Boards—How to Get Rebounds

Fact: Most shots in a basketball game are missed.

Fact: The team that grabs most of those misses—known as rebounds—will usually win.

There are two kinds of rebounds, offensive and defensive. Defensive rebounds result when your opponents miss a shot, offensive rebounds when your own team misses. The better job you do at defensive rebounding, the fewer shots the opponents get—and the fewer their opportunities to score. They need the ball to score and you're reducing their time of possession.

On the other side, the better job you do at offensive rebounding, the more shots you have—and the more chances to score. Say your team sinks 50 percent of its shots from the field. If you take 36 shots in a game, that comes to 18 baskets, or 36 points. Now let's say you crash the offensive boards, and get an extra 12 shots—totaling 48 for the game. If you shoot at the same 50-percent rate (and you'd probably shoot better, because shots off rebounds are higher-percentage shots since they come from close in), your point total is up to 48 points. That 12-point increase could well mean the difference between victory and defeat.

Not only is rebounding a vital strategic element of the game, it's also fun. For me, there are few moments on the court that compare to the feeling of pulling down a rebound with authority. Everyone's going for the ball, but you go up and claim it for yourself. It gives you a sense of power and control, and makes you feel as though you're really a force on the court.

Who Wants It?

Good rebounders usually are tall. Often they are fine jumpers. They are always players with desire. They want the ball more than anyone else, and that means they work harder to get it. A former player of mine at Manhattan College, Sheila Tighe, is a great example of how far desire goes under the boards. At 5-foot-9, Sheila went up against a lot of taller players and better leapers. But she always went to the boards hard—and always got more than her share of rebounds.

Obviously certain physical limitations come into play here. No matter how much you want the ball, if you're 5-foot-1 you're just not going to get it very often. The important thing to remember is that you can be a good rebounder if you really want to be, even if you're just an average-sized player or only a fair jumper.

Defensive Rebounding

The easiest way to lose a game is to allow your opponents two or three shots at the hoop each time they move down the floor. Sound work on the defensive boards is the only way to stop that from happening.

The key to defensive rebounding is boxing out. Also called blocking out or screening out, this maneuver involves using your body to keep your opponent behind you so you'll have the all-important inside position for the rebound. It's very tempting when you see a shot go up to forget about your opponent and simply go for the ball. Resist the temptation if you really want the rebound. If you don't box out your opponent she has a chance to slip inside you and get first try at the ball. Sooner or later it'll cost you.

Keeping Your Opponent Away

When your opponent takes a shot, the first thing you should do is to yell, "Shot!" This alerts everyone on your team that it's time to box out. Once the shot is taken, check your opponent to see which way she's moving. (If she's not moving, she's doing you a big favor. Then all you have to do is pivot and get into rebounding position.) If she's cutting to your left, execute a forward pivot: leading with your chest, use your left foot as a pivot and bring your right foot around so you wind up squarely in her path and facing the basket. If she's cutting to your right, forward pivot with your right foot as the pivot. Again, pivot chest first, bringing your left foot around

Fig. 11–1 Boxing Out. As the offensive player makes a move to the basket *(left)*, the defender makes a forward pivot, stepping directly into her path to keep her away from the basket *(right)*. Always box out on defense. Giving away the inside position is almost as bad as giving away the rebound.

in the same way, so you're facing the basket and your opponent is behind you.

Keep a wide base, both to improve your balance and to obstruct her path to the basket. For the best position, move your feet at least a foot wider than your shoulders, and keep your elbows well away from your body and your hands up, ready to gain possession. Your rear end should be down and your knees should be well-flexed so you're prepared to jump when the ball comes off the boards. Make contact with your opponent as soon as you box her out so you keep track of where she is and maintain the inside position.

If she's a determined offensive rebounder, she'll continue trying to get past you. Don't let her. You can't see exactly where she's going because she is behind you and you're now looking for the ball coming off the rim. So you have to "feel" for her with your upper arms, back, and backside, shuffling with short, choppy steps to cut her off whichever way she's moving. Keep your feet moving to reestablish your position when she tries to slip past you. If all this sounds like hard work, you're right. But it doesn't last long; usually you have to maintain the inside position for only a few seconds before the ball is in someone's possession.

The Right Way to Rebound

Okay, you've done a good job boxing out. You've staked out your inside

Fig. 11–2 Pulling down a rebound. The rebounder is in good position *(top left).* Her knees are flexed, she's well-balanced and her hands are up, waiting for the ball to come off. She goes up strongly for the ball, reaching high and extending her body to its fullest *(top right).* She brings it down, holding it firmly with her elbows out slightly for protection *(bottom left),* then pivots to the outside to throw an outlet pass *(bottom right).*

position, taking up as much space as you can with a low, wide stance and with your elbows out. You've established contact with your opponent and you're ready to react. Now it's time to go up and get the basketball.

Timing is critical in rebounding. Jump a second early or late and you're not going to get the ball. That means you must be poised to jump the moment it comes off the rim. Maintain a wide base and keep your knees flexed. Stay on the balls of your feet and keep your feet moving, even if they remain in more or less the same spot. When they're already in motion it's easier to get them off the floor quickly.

As the ball descends, time your jump so you'll get to it at your highest jump level. Explode upward from your coiled stance with a forceful push from the balls of your feet and extend your arms to their fullest. Grab the ball with authority, bringing it in toward your chest with both hands. Come down with your legs apart (it will give you more floor space once you're down) and land on the balls of your feet with your body well balanced. Hold the ball tightly and keep your elbows out to discourage anyone from stealing it. Just be sure not to swing your elbows; that's a flagrant foul that could cause a serious injury.

Now that you've done the hard part and pulled in the rebound, don't panic. Rushing the release of the ball is asking for a turnover. Pivot away from the basket, where it's both congested and dangerous, and look to make an outlet pass to a teammate in the flat—the area between the free-throw line, extended, and the baseline. If a teammate isn't there, yell, "Help!" and someone should move quickly into a safe passing range and angle. Avoid passing to the middle or across the court; these passes won't get past an alert defender. It is much better to pause a moment or two while a guard gets open, then throw a safe pass.

Dribble only as a last resort. If it is necessary, make it a low, power drib-

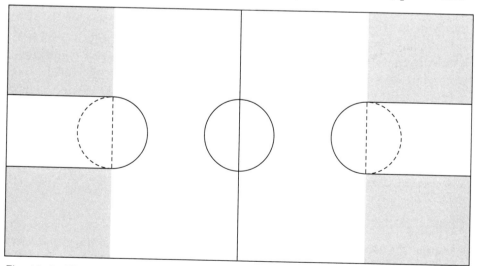

Fig. 11–3 The flats, shown by the shading, are where outlet passes usually are thrown.

ble to safeguard it from the defense. You shouldn't need more than three bounces to reach a safe area. Don't get carried away. There are few things a coach hates more than a player doing a great job of getting a rebound, only to give it up by overdribbling.

Offensive Rebounding

Defensive rebounding is hard work. Offensive rebounding is even harder, for two reasons. One, you're farther from the basket, and two, you have to get around your opponent to get the inside position (whereas a defender usually has it).

But hitting the offensive boards is worth it for one very big reason. When you get the ball on a rebound, you're usually no more than a foot or two from the hoop. Lay-up country. Who doesn't like an easy two?

To be an effective offensive rebounder, you've got to go hard to the boards every time, and you've got to do it the moment you see that a shot is going up. She who hesitates is lost. Anticipate when a shot will be released. Know your teammates and when and where each likes to shoot; that way you know when to go to the boards. Make a sharp, direct cut (if it's available) to the basket. Suppose your team's best shooter has the ball and is wide open from 15 feet out. You know the ball's going up so you go to the basket right away. By getting a split-second jump on the defender, you can sneak inside before she has a chance to box you out.

If you do get boxed out, try to get around her. Be relentless. Cut one way, then another. Fake that you're trying to beat her to the right, then change direction and go to the left. Keep moving in any case; don't get caught watching the flight of the ball. Watching won't get you any rebounds, but moving will, and even if you don't succeed in getting the inside position, all your activity may distract your opponent enough to allow one of your teammates to get the ball.

Sometimes you may be able to touch the ball, but not grab it with both hands. If that's the case, try to tip it in the air. Keep it alive—and away from your opponent. Contest every rebound. If you can't get inside your defender, at least get beside her. Go hard to the boards every time. Aggressive offensive rebounding puts constant pressure on the defense, and if you keep at it you're going to get the ball a good share of the time. Nothing demoralizes the opposition quite like playing good defense, forcing a missed shot, only to have you sneak in, grab an offensive rebound and make an easy basket.

Hints for Good Rebounding

• Assume that every shot is going to miss. If you don't, you'll lose a few vital moments that may mean not getting the rebound. On defense, box out and get into proper rebounding stance on every shot. On offense, go to

the boards until you see the ball drop or until the other team gets it.
- Don't watch the flight of the ball. I promise, the shooter is aiming in the direction of the goal. Watching can cost you that extra step which, again, could well be the difference between getting the ball and not getting it. It's a common mistake to follow the ball and hope it comes to where you're standing. Much better to move into prime rebounding position, where the ball usually comes off, and go after it from there.
- Don't get too far underneath the basket. We just talked about prime rebounding position. What is that? Many players think it's right under the basket, figuring the closer you are, the better the position. Not true. Being three feet out is better than being 13 feet out, but if you get caught directly beneath the basket, you're not going to grab anything but the ball as it falls through the net. Optimum position is about three to four feet—a giant step—away from the basket.
- A valuable statistic to keep in mind: The ball rebounds to the opposite side of the basket more than 75 percent of the time. Thus if a shot is taken to the left of the lane, chances are very good it'll come off to the right.
- When you're going for a defensive rebound, try to coordinate with your teammates so you've got the three prime areas around the basket—left, right, and middle—covered. It does no good for two of you to be standing right on top of each other while another area is wide open.
- Defense isn't over until your team has possession of the ball. Unaccountably, some teams seem to relax as soon as they see a shot missed (those are bad rebounding teams, I guarantee you). A good offensive rebounding team will destroy them.
- Defensive rebounding, especially, is a team responsibility. If three people work hard and box out properly, it won't do the team much good if a fourth doesn't, because it could well be her player who gets the ball. Nobody can afford to take a holiday on the defensive boards.
- Jump! If you're flat-footed when the ball goes up, or if you're not in a well-coiled stance, the rebound is going to be someone else's. You must be ready to jump, to spring toward the ball with a powerful upward thrust.
- Be aggressive. Somebody once said that basketball is a non-contact sport. That somebody was wrong. Be aggressive when you're rebounding. Go after the ball hard, and grab it with authority. Don't worry about making incidental contact with other players. Body contact is a part of the game under the boards.
- Don't climb over anyone's back. Along with the reach-in foul, a favorite call among officials seems to be "over the top," which occurs when a player on the outside climbs on the back of the player in front of her. Go up straight for the ball. Jump up, not forward, and you shouldn't have any problem with the whistle-blowers.
- When you get an offensive rebound, go right back up with it—and go up strong. Sure, it's crowded and physical in there, but you lose a big advantage if you take your rebound and dribble or pass to a clearer area. Put

the ball right back up—and do it without dribbling, if possible, since a dribble is liable to get deflected or stolen. If you're too closely guarded to get off a good shot, give a quick, upward fake with your head and shoulders, pretending you're going up for the shot. When the defenders go for the fake and leave their feet, wait for them to begin coming down, then go up for the shot. You stand a good chance of making an easy basket, and a great chance of drawing a foul and possibly getting a three-point play.

• On the offensive boards, if you can't grab it, tip it. Do anything you can to prevent the other team from securing possession. If the ball stays alive long enough, maybe one of your teammates will be the one to pull it out of the air and put it in.

• Keep your hands up and elbows out, taking up as much space as possible. Extend fully as you go after the ball.

• If you've pulled down a defensive rebound and don't have a ready outlet pass, hold the ball firmly and keep it moving close to your body. The best way to stop the opposition from tying you up is by keeping the ball active.

• Stay with it. Great rebounders are relentless. They go to the boards every chance they get. They refuse to give up. They're constantly on the move. Good rebounding requires a lot of hard work, but it's effort well spent.

Rebounding Drills

Box-Out

A coach or player takes a 15- to 20-foot shot while two or three (or even one) defenders turn and box out their opponents, who are trying for the offensive rebound. The defense has to get the rebound on three consecutive shots before the offense and defense switch.

Animal Drill

A great way to work on rebounding aggressively and going up with power. Three players take rebounding positions near the basket. A shot is taken, and it's every girl for herself. Little bumps are allowed, and each player goes for the ball. The two who do not get it immediately turn and must defend the player who did. The girl with the ball must go straight up with it; only two dribbles are allowed. Play continues until someone puts in a rebound. Then bring the ball back out to the shooter and repeat the drill, playing until one player has five baskets.

Three-Way Drill

Player A tosses the ball high off the left side of the backboard (an intentional miss) and pulls down the rebound herself. She turns to the outside and passes to Player B, who breaks to the flat for the outlet pass. A follows her pass, then B dribbles in and tosses the ball way up on the board as A

Fig. 11–4 Three-way re-bounding drill. O_3 tosses the ball up on the board, gets her own rebound and snaps off an outlet pass to O_1. O_3 follows her pass, and O_1 dribbles in to the right side of the lane, tosses it up and rebounds in sim-ilar fashion, makes an out-let to O_2, then follows her pass. O_2 dribbles in to the left side, tosses it up, re-bounds and makes the outlet to O_3. The pattern continues until each player has pulled down ten re-bounds.

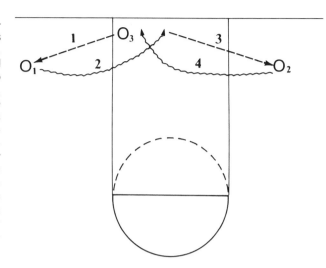

did, gets the rebound, and passes to Player C, on the right side, who fol-lows the same pattern. Run it through so each player gets 10 rebounds. Work on planting yourself, jumping with power, and extending your body as high as you can as you forcefully grab the rebound out of the air.

A Final Word

I once coached a player who always worked hard to do things the right way, and rebounding was no exception. She boxed out effectively, kept a good, low position, the whole bit. She protected the ball well, made good outlet passes—everything was fundamentally sound.

But you know what? She wasn't a great rebounder. Not because she did anything fundamentally wrong, but because she didn't have the take-charge, this-ball-is-mine mentality that is the hallmark of a really good rebounder.

It's competitive under there; a lot of people want that ball, and if it's going to be yours, you're just going to have to go after it harder than any-body else.

This isn't to say that the techniques and hints we've looked at are not im-portant; they're absolutely essential. But technique alone will not get you the ball. You have to want it, and you have to go and get it. Let the opposi-tion know you're going to fight for every single board. Let them know you're not going to quit, that you won't allow them to relax. You're constantly going to be on the move. With this sort of attitude, coupled with the fun-damentals we've looked at in this chapter, you'll be a rebounder to reckon with.

Chapter Twelve

All About Zones

Chances are good you will play, or play against, a zone defense quite often as you get involved in organized basketball. There are many different kinds of zones and an equal number of ways to attack them. Getting into the strategic specifics of each is not our concern here. Rather, let's look at how zones work and how to play them defensively—and attack them offensively—for best results.

What Is a Zone?

In a man-to-man defense, your responsibility is to guard a specific player, whom you defend wherever she goes (and, of course, to provide support to your teammates if they need it). In a zone defense, your assignment is not one player but a particular area (or zone) of the court. You must guard any player who moves into the zone you're responsible for. When that player cuts to another part of the court, someone else must pick her up. The zone shifts as the ball moves from one offensive player to another, enabling the defense to stop the players who are the most threatening at that moment. As a rule, when the ball isn't in your area, you sag into the lane to make it more difficult for the offense to penetrate the zone.

Why Play a Zone?

A zone defense offers several advantages. Foremost is that it can be a good way to stop an opponent's inside game. By packing five players into the free-throw lane, a defensive team makes it very difficult for the offense to penetrate for high-percentage shots. Say you're playing against a team with a high-scoring center. To try to stop her, a coach may go to a tight 2–3 zone, which would position two players at the free-throw line, and three across

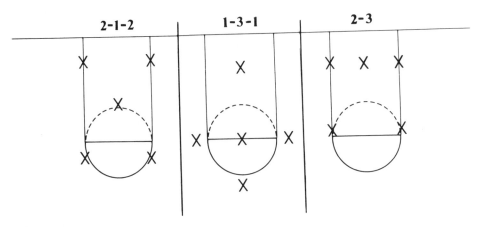

Fig. 12–1 Three common zone defenses: the 2–1–2, 1–3–1, and the 2–3.

the bottom of the key. The guards would collapse into the middle either to prevent the dangerous center from getting the ball or, if she does get it, to make it as difficult as possible for her to score or make a threatening pass.

Zones are especially effective against teams with poor outside shooters. The less the zone has to worry about the outside shot, the more it can stay in tight and virtually shut off the area closer to the basket.

Other advantages of a zone are:

• It works well against an impatient team. Often a team must work the ball around to get a good shot against a zone. If the offensive team lacks discipline and doesn't take the time to move the ball, the zone can present huge problems for it.

• It can keep players out of foul trouble. Consistently playing man-to-man often results in a lot of personal fouls. In a zone, where the defensive responsibility isn't on a single player, a defender isn't as likely to incur that problem. That's why a coach frequently will go to a zone if a key player picks up a couple of quick fouls or is in danger of fouling out of the game.

• It can "hide" a weak defensive player. A weak defensive link is very easy for a good offensive team to exploit in a man-to-man defense. It can simply continue to pass the ball to the player being guarded by the weak defender. But when that defender is part of a zone, her weaknesses are not quite so glaring because she's guarding an area of the court, and her teammates can help her out more readily. Thus the opponents cannot take advantage of her in the same way.

• It can help a team establish good rebounding position. In the 2–3, for instance, three players, when in their normal defensive areas, already are stationed in good rebounding position. Because they remain in those areas there's never a chance that one of your team's main rebounders might be twenty feet from the basket, as there is when she's guarding someone man-to-man.

Disadvantages of Zone Defenses

There are also inherent weaknesses in zones. The main one is that, because players are responsible for an area and not a single opponent, there will be in-between areas, or "seams," where it's uncertain who has the defensive responsibility. First-rate zone defenses can counteract this problem with quick, aggressive shifts, but most teams will be vulnerable in these areas.

A zone generally will not be useful against a good passing team, one that moves the ball quickly around the court. Against this sort of ball movement, it's very difficult for the zone to shift quickly enough to stay well positioned. A skillful, patient offensive team can simply work the ball around until the zone begins breaking down as players get tired or lose concentration.

Different zones have different weaknesses, but any zone set-up will be burned by a team of good outside shooters. Usually a few quick passes around the perimeter are all that's necessary to get an open jumper. A team that hits those shots forces the zone to come farther out. The inside areas that were so packed with defenders before become easier to penetrate by the offense. Sometimes you'll see games where a coach opens up in a zone defense to challenge the opponent to shoot from the outside. If the team can't make the perimeter shots the coach will stay with her zone. But if the opponent is accurate from outside, usually the coach will abandon the zone and go to a man-to-man, which will put more pressure on the ball.

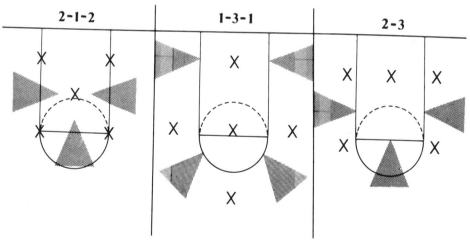

Fig. 12–2 Each player has an area of responsibility in a zone defense. The areas between the defenders, called the seams, are where the zone is weakest and where the zone should be attacked.

Things to Keep in Mind When Playing in a Zone

Here are some important points to remember when playing in a zone defense:

• Get back on defense and set up the zone quickly. This way you'll be ready to stop the opposing team even if they try to fast-break. Zones are weakened if every player doesn't hustle into her defensive position.

• Some players play a zone as though it relieves them of all defensive responsibility. All the principles we discussed in our chapter on defense still apply when you're playing a zone. Stay low with your knees flexed and move quickly with short, choppy steps. Zones constantly are shifting as the offense moves the ball. You must keep moving, and if you're standing up straight you won't be able to move as effectively. Always know where the ball is. Keep your arms up (particularly when the ball isn't in your area) to make it harder for the offense to penetrate and to see the passing lanes.

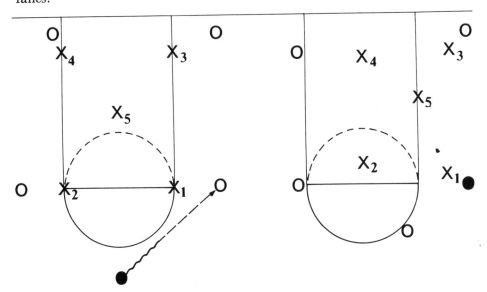

Fig. 12–3　An example of how a 2–1–2 zone shifts when the ball moves. Notice how, with the ball on the wing, players X_1 and X_3 move outward to put more pressure on the ball, while players away from the ball, particularly X_4, sag into the middle to keep the zone tight.

• Talk! Communication is vital to any defensive scheme, but probably most of all in a zone. Keep talking to avoid confusion about defensive assignments. "I got her," "Pick her up," "Coming your way," "Watch the cutter" are common ways of helping one another out.

• Keep moving and play aggressively so the ball stays on the perimeter. Don't let the ball get in the middle of the zone. That's where you're most vulnerable because once an opponent gets the ball in there she'll have a good chance for a high-percentage shot or have several open passing lanes to teammates. If the ball does get in the key, "pinch in" down low and tighten the zone to cut off easy passing lanes.

• Be aware of the offense's habits and which players are the greatest scoring threats. Suppose the opponent's high-scorer, a great outside shooter, is setting up in your part of the zone. You'll want to put extra pressure on her so she won't get a high-percentage shot. You may play her in a denial defense, making it impossible for her to get the ball anywhere near her shooting range. With you playing farther out from your usual zone position, your teammates might compensate by shifting a step toward you. This will help cover your area and reduce her passing options while still keeping the zone tight.

- Keep the opponents off the boards. Boxing out is just as important in a zone as in a man-to-man defense. You can't just turn and go for the rebound, because an offensive player is liable to slip into an inside position. Block out any opponent in your area before you go for the rebound.
- "Bump" all the cutters. Lane denial is as important in zones as it is in a man-to-man defense. Often the offense against your zone will send cutters through the middle. Try to slow them down by stepping into their path, forcing them either low (toward the baseline) or high (above the free-throw line), depending on where the ball is. If the ball is low, force them to go high; if it's high, make them go low. That way they're always forced away from the ball—where it's harder for them to receive it. They can stay in the free-throw lane for only three seconds, so you only have to bump them for a moment to disrupt their cut—and the flow of the offense.

Things to Keep in Mind When Playing Offense Against a Zone

- Play up-tempo basketball. Fast-break if you have the chance, but even if you can't go all the way to the basket, push the ball upcourt quickly. A good way to attack a zone is to do so before it gets set up.
- Keep the ball moving. Don't pass the ball once or twice and throw up a low-percentage outside shot. That's playing into the zone's hands. Be patient. Work the ball around from side to side. Make them work to keep up with you. Before long you'll see the zone isn't moving as well, and the result will be better opportunities to shoot or pass the ball inside.
- Try to penetrate the middle, where the zone is most vulnerable. Probe for defensive weaknesses—players who are out of position or making improper shifts. Look for teammates cutting through the zone. Try to get the ball into the high post. If you get the ball inside consistently, you'll get high-percentage shots, and should beat the zone every time.
- Don't dribble unless it's necessary. Dribbling slows down ball movement, making it easier for the zone to defend you. Keep the ball off the floor unless you're driving to the basket, improving a passing angle, or need to get away from pressure. This rule applies all the time, but especially when you're in the lane—where you're surrounded by defenders and the ball is easy to steal.
- Reverse the zone. This means passing the ball in one direction, then quickly reversing the flow and going back the other way. For instance, suppose

the point guard passes to the left wing and the zone shifts over in that direction. To reverse the zone, the left wing passes back to the point, who moves it quickly to the right wing. As another option, the wing might skip over the guard and throw an overhead pass to the opposite forward. Either way, this simple reversal frequently will catch the defense in transition and lead to a wide-open shot, particularly if the defense tends to overplay the ball.

• Always face the basket and get into triple-threat position when you receive the ball. Make the defense respect all your options.

• Fake and pass. Fakes are a good way to create weaknesses in the zone, particularly an aggressive one that is playing the passing lanes. A good fake to the right, then a quick pass to the left can have the same effect as reversing the zone. It can make the entire defense overextend in the wrong direction.

• Look for the skip pass. If the defense shifts a lot and overplays the ball, the skip pass probably will be open. A skip pass is an overhead pass that's thrown to a teammate two or more players away. By skipping over the teammate closest to you, you move the ball so quickly that the defense can't shift fast enough to stay in good position.

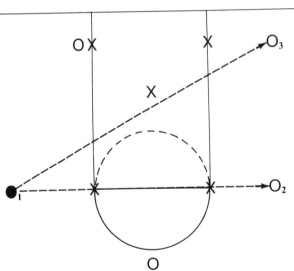

Fig. 12–4 The skip pass is an overhead pass made to a teammate two or more regular passes away from the ball. In the diagram, O_1 has the ball. By skip passing to either O_2 or O_3, O_1 may catch the defense in transition and create an opportunity for an open shot.

• Stay composed. Be patient. Move the ball, look for the open player and keep the defense occupied with lots of sharp passes and cuts. The better the ball movement, the better the chance the zone will become overextended or out of position. Many teams lose because they shoot too quickly against a tight zone defense.

• Always look to attack the seams of the zone, those in-between areas where it's uncertain whose territory it is to cover. Good ball movement often will create openings at the seams, giving you a good opportunity to penetrate the middle of the zone.

• The guard who initiates the offense must force the defense to actively play her; otherwise the zone can stay tight, play the passing lanes, and guard your four remaining players with its five players. If you're starting the offense, dribble toward the defense until they play you, then pass the ball off. If the defense doesn't pick you up, keep going to the basket or pull up for a short jumper. The idea is to challenge them, make them play you right off the bat, because it'll open up the passing lanes to begin your offense.

A Final Word

The middle area is the key to a zone defense. When your team is using the zone, your top priority is to keep the zone tight and the middle well-guarded so you take away the opponent's inside game. Force them to beat you from outside. Bump cutters through the zone away from the ball so they can't hurt you inside. By moving well and keeping the zone tight, you often make the opposing team impatient and frustrated, and the result is that they'll take a low-percentage shot or try to force the ball inside, often leading to a turnover.

When you're playing against a zone, you don't want to fall victim to such impatience. Work the ball around. Reverse the zone. Keep the ball moving, throw crisp passes, and avoid unnecessary dribbling. Gradually the zone coverage will break down. Stay alert, constantly looking for openings in the middle. Always remember: *Good ball movement is the key to beating the zone.* They can't shift as fast as you can pass, and the result will be the shooting and passing opportunities you're looking for.

Chapter Thirteen

Parting Thoughts

Keeping It Simple

We've talked a lot of basketball in this book, but if there's just one more piece of advice I'd like to send you away with it's this: Keep it simple.

Some of the things we've talked about are complicated. But the players who perform the best—and improve the fastest—are the ones who stick to the basics, who work on playing the game soundly and simply. The best way is the simplest way, which is why I've stressed the importance of eliminating wasted motion from your game. It only complicates things. Why take a long, looping path to the basket when a simple, direct cut would be much more effective? Why make a bunch of halfhearted fakes when trying to get in for an offensive rebound, when one sharp change of direction probably would do the trick? Why shoot with your elbow out from your body and compensate for it by spinning the ball from the side? Some players succeed with unorthodox shooting styles, but they're the exceptions. Keep it simple. Keep your elbow in line with the foot, knee, and hip as we discussed and release the ball directly toward the basket with a nice, straight backspin. Simplicity breeds consistency.

Concentrate on mastering the fundamentals. Execute them with the proper technique. Keeping it simple will make your basketball more fun and your results more impressive, and give you a firm foundation for improvement. Even the most spectacular plays are just extensions of the game's fundamentals.

Here are some other thoughts, suggestions, and reminders about how to approach the game.

Giving It Your Best

Playing basketball has given me personal satisfaction as well as many great experiences. The game has paid my way through college, given me the opportunity to meet lots of people, and let me travel extensively and write this book.

Your level of commitment to the game is up to you. Not everybody is cut out to be an all-American, and not everybody wants to be. Maybe you aspire to play in a top collegiate program, or maybe you're happy to have made the high school JV. Whatever your goals in playing may be, make the time you put into basketball quality time. Try your best and work your hardest. As with everything else you do, that's the only way if you want to walk away feeling good about your effort and your accomplishments.

Good Nights and Bad

The best pros have bad games and practice sessions. You will, too, and if you keep that in mind they'll be easier to handle when they come. Always strive for perfection, but don't get down because you don't attain it. Aim high, push yourself to improve, and keep in mind that the challenge is what makes it fun. Sometimes you'll feel as though you're not measuring up to the challenge the way you want to, but you can't worry about yesterday's missed shot or fumbled pass. When things aren't going well, the best thing you can do is to learn from it, and go out the next day with a clear head so you can focus all your mental and physical energy on getting back on track.

Getting Playing Time

Only five players can play at once, and most teams carry at least ten or twelve. The result is that often there isn't enough playing time to keep everybody happy. If you're not getting the time you'd like, if you feel your abilities are not appreciated or are going to waste, bear in mind that absolutely the worst thing to do is sulk about it. That won't do anything except alienate you from the coach and your teammates.

Keep working hard in practice. Make your coach aware that your attitude and commitment to the team are solid. This isn't easy when you feel slighted, but it's the only way to go.

It's also a good idea to let your coach know your feelings. Seek her out and ask for her honest appraisal of your ability, your place on the team and what fundamentals you need to improve. What should you work on? What specifically can you do that might enhance your value to the team and get you more time? Most coaches will respect you for being mature enough and concerned enough to talk with them in this way. You're the only one with the power to change your coach's thinking about your place on the team, and the way to start is with a positive attitude and a lot of hard work in practice.

It's a Team Game

How well your team fares depends on how the individual talents blend together into a cohesive unit. How enjoyable and satisfying your season is depends largely on how much everyone pulls together. Your basketball experiences will be more rewarding if you strive always to be a good team player, on the court and off.

What is a good team player? She is unselfish. She passes up her own open shot to give the ball to an open teammate closer to the basket. She also passes kind words, praising good efforts by her teammates and offering encouragement whenever needed. She is positive and supportive, and is often heard saying, "Nice going" and "Hang in there." She is able to admit when she's at fault. She works hard in practice and always gives 100 percent, even if she isn't a star of the team. She's alert and attentive, asks questions and always listens to her coach. She doesn't gossip behind anybody's back because she knows how easily resentments and ill feelings can spread—and spoil everybody's fun.

More than anything else, the good team player brings her enthusiasm with her every day, from tryouts right through to the last game of the season. She's upbeat, she looks on the positive side, and she has fun as she's playing the game hard. She cares enough to share her enthusiasm, and she knows when you give something positive to others it always comes back to you. She also knows the truth of something we touched on at the very beginning of this book, and that's a good place to end: Nothing great was ever achieved without enthusiasm.

Glossary

assist   A pass that results in a score by a teammate.

backboard   The rectangular board behind the basket used for shooting bank shots.

backcourt   The half of the court containing the basket that a team is defending.

back door   A cut behind the defender that a player uses when she is being overplayed.

bank shot   A carom shot in which the backboard is used.

baseball pass   A pass thrown with the same overhand motion used to throw a baseball or softball. Used primarily to advance the ball a long way downcourt.

baseline   The line behind each basket marking the end of the court.

basket   The goal players shoot for to score points. Also, a shot that goes through the goal.

bounce pass   A pass that touches the floor before reaching its receiver.

boxing out   A blocking move a player uses to gain and keep the inside rebounding position by keeping her opponent behind her. Also called blocking out.

carry   A violation committed when a player cradles the ball and momentarily holds it while dribbling. Also called palming.

center   A position usually played by the tallest player and best rebounder on the team. The center normally sets up in the center of the court close to the basket, around the free-throw lane.

charging   A violation committed when an offensive player runs into a stationary defensive player.

chest pass   A two-handed pass thrown from the passer's chest to the chest area of the receiver.

combination defense   A defense employing elements of both zone and man-to-man defenses.

cut A sharp move made by an offensive player in order to get open or to beat a defender.

defense The team that attempts to keep its opponent from scoring.

defensive rebound A rebound at the basket you're defending.

denial A defensive tactic used to prevent an opponent from getting the ball.

double dribble A violation caused by starting to dribble, stopping, and then dribbling a second time.

double-teaming A tactic in which two defensive players guard one offensive player, usually the one with the ball.

dribble The bouncing movement of the ball—the only way an offensive player is permitted to move with the ball.

drive A quick offensive move toward the basket with the dribble.

elbow The court area where the free-throw line meets the side of the key.

fake A body movement used to draw a defender out of position.

fast break A style of play in which a team moves the ball upcourt as quickly as possible after a rebound or steal in hopes of gaining a quick advantage on the defense and getting an easy shot.

field goal A basket scored on any shot other than a free throw. Worth two points.

flat The area of the court from the baseline to the free-throw line extended; where outlet passes are usually thrown.

forecourt The half of the court containing the basket the offensive team is shooting for. Also known as the frontcourt.

forward A position usually played by taller players who set up to the sides of the basket and relatively close to it.

foul A violation caused by illegal contact with an opposing player; can result in free throws for the opponent.

free-throw An unguarded shot taken from the free-throw line after an opponent has committed a foul. A successful free throw counts for one point.

free-throw lane See "key."

fronting Defending an opponent by positioning your body between her and the ball.

give and go An offensive play in which a player passes to a teammate and cuts toward the basket looking for a return pass.

guard A position usually played by smaller, quicker players who are good ball handlers. Normally a guard sets up on the perimeter, well away from the basket.

helping out Assisting a teammate in defensive coverage.

high post A position around the free-throw line played by a center or forward.

jab step A short, quick foot fake used to set up a defender for a drive or shot.

jump ball The procedure for starting play at the beginning or during a game in which an official tosses the ball into the air; two opposing players jump up and try to tap it to a teammate.

jump shot   An outside shot taken by a player after she has jumped into the air.

key   The six-foot-wide area between the free-throw line and the baseline. Also called the free-throw lane.

lay-up   A close-in shot usually banked off the backboard.

low post   A position near the basket played by a center, usually with her back to the basket.

man-to-man defense   A type of defense in which each player has a specific opposing player to defend.

off hand   The weaker hand. For right-handed players, the left hand; for left-handers, the right.

offense   The team that has the ball and is attempting to score.

offensive rebound   A rebound at the basket you're team is shooting at.

one on one   Any situation in which one offensive player attempts to score on her defensive opponent.

outlet pass   A pass (usually an overhead pass to the flat) made by a rebounder to a teammate in order to start the offensive flow. Very important to a successful fast break.

overhead pass   A two-handed pass thrown from over the head.

overplaying defense   An aggressive defense in which players gamble to steal the ball or deny it to the offense.

passing lane   The imaginary path between a passer and her teammate.

pivot   Footwork in which a player swivels on one foot and moves the other forward or backward.

point guard   The guard designated as the "quarterback" of the offense. She usually brings the ball upcourt and handles it more than any other player.

possession   A term describing when a team has the ball.

rebound   A missed shot that bounces off the backboard or basket. Also the act of taking possession of a missed shot.

reversing a zone   Moving the ball against a zone defense quickly from one side of the court to the other. Often results in an open shot because the defense cannot keep up.

roll   A move executed by a player setting a screen in which she pivots toward the ball so that she's in a position to receive a pass.

screen   A block an offensive player sets against a defender to free another offensive player for a shot or pass. Also called a pick.

skip pass   An overhead pass that is thrown to a teammate two or more players away; used to exploit a zone.

squaring up   A move in which a player pivots and squarely faces the basket after receiving the ball.

strong side   The side of the court where the ball is.

three seconds   A violation in which an offensive player remains in the key for more than three consecutive seconds.

trailer   An offensive player, usually a rebounder, who follows behind the play on a fast break.

traveling   A violation committed when a player takes steps with the ball without dribbling. Also called walking.

triple-threat position   A stance taken by an offensive player upon receiving the ball that gives her the option to shoot, pass, or dribble.

turnover   Any ball-handling error or violation (for example, making a bad pass or traveling) that gives possession of the ball to the opposing team.

weak side   The side of the court where the ball isn't; when the ball is on the left, the weak side is the right.

zone defense   A type of defense in which players guard a particular area of the court rather than a specific opposing player.

Index